Elizabeth Mestheneos, Judy T
on behalf of the EUROFAMC

Supporting Family Carers of Older
The Pan-European Backgr

CU00558496

Supporting Family Carers of Older People in Europe

Empirical Evidence, Policy Trends and Future Perspectives

edited by

Hanneli Döhner and Christopher Kofahl
University of Hamburg

vol. 1

LIT

Elizabeth Mestheneos, Judy Triantafillou
on behalf of the EUROFAMCARE group

Supporting Family Carers of Older People in Europe – The Pan-European Background Report

LIT

This report is part of the European Union funded project
"Services for Supporting Family Carers of Elderly People in Europe:
Characteristics, Coverage and Usage" – EUROFAMCARE
EUROFAMCARE is an international research project funded within the
5th Framework Programme of the European Community,
Key Action 6: The Ageing Population and Disabilities,
6.5: Health and Social Care Services to older People,
Contract N° QLK6-CT-2002-02647 "EUROFAMCARE"
http://www.uke.uni-hamburg.de/eurofamcare
All rights by the authors and the EUROFAMCARE-consortium.

EUROFAMCARE is co-ordinated by the

University Medical Centre Hamburg-Eppendorf,
Institute for Medical Sociology,
Dr. Hanneli Döhner
Martinistr. 52
20246 Hamburg
Germany
doehner@uke.uni-hamburg.de

This report reflects the authors' view. It does not necessarily reflect the European
Commission's view and in no way anticipates its future policy in this area.
Designed and edited by Christopher Kofahl
Final Layout: Maik Philipp, Florian Lüdeke, Christopher Kofahl

Bibliographic information published by Die Deutsche Bibliothek
Die Deutsche Bibliothek lists this publication in the Deutsche
Nationalbibliografie; detailed bibliographic data are available in the
Internet at http://dnb.ddb.de.

ISBN 3-8258-9121-6

A catalogue record for this book is available from the British Library

© LIT VERLAG Münster   2005
Grevener Str./Fresnostr. 2   D- 48159 Münster
Tel. +49/(0)251-62 03 20   Fax +49/(0)251-23 19 72
e-Mail: lit@lit-verlag.de   http://www.lit-verlag.de

Distributed in the UK by: Global Book Marketing, 38 King Street, London WC 2E 8JT
Phone: +44 (0) 207 240 6649 – Fax: +44 (0) 20 7497 0309, http://www.globalbookmarketing.co.uk

Distributed in North America by:

Transaction Publishers
New Brunswick (U.S.A.) and London (U.K.)

Transaction Publishers
Rutgers University
35 Berrue Circle
Piscataway, NJ 08854

Tel.: (732) 445 - 2280
Fax: (732) 445 - 3138
for orders (U. S. only):
toll free (888) 999 - 6778

Content

Preface by the Editors:
A Short Description of EUROFAMCARE

EUROFAMCARE is the acronym of the project "Services for Supporting Family Carers of Elderly People in Europe: Characteristics, Coverage and Usage" funded by the EU within the 5th Framework Programme "Quality of Life and Management of Living Resources". As part of the Key Action 6: The Ageing Population and Disabilities; 6.5: Health and Social Care Services to older People it aims to provide a European review of the situation of family carers of elderly people in relation to the existence, familiarity, availability, use and acceptability of supporting services.

Six-Country Study

In the year 2003 six countries (Germany, Greece, Italy, Poland, Sweden, United Kingdom) have formed a trans-European group, systematically representing the different types of welfare-states in Europe and started a comparative study. Each country collected data from about 1,000 family carers who care at least four hours a week for their dependent elderly (65+) family members in different regional sites. The family carers were interviewed face-to-face at home using a joint family care assessment.

The views of potential service providers involved were obtained in the year 2004. Quantitative and qualitative data of these interviews were entered in National Data Sets and a European data base for cross-national analysis. A typology of care settings will be developed considering examples of good practice and beneficial and obstructive circumstances.

Pan-European Review

Pan-European expertise, knowledge and background information about the support, relief and expertise of family carers recognising the variety of the different social-, health- and welfare systems in a future Europe have been achieved by reviews and expert interviews in the six project countries plus 17 further European countries.

AGE – the European Older People's Platform – as a member of the consortium is contacting and informing policy makers and NGOs on the European level and measuring the development of action for family carers. AGE aims to raise more awareness about the issue of family care and to stimulate the political discourse.

Socio-Economics

A socio-economic evaluation on the basis of the National Surveys and the pan-European background information will calculate the economic consequences from perceived quality of life to European-wide politico-economic implications.

Transfer and Dissemination

The last step is a feedback research action phase based both on the study results and on the pan-European expertise. A European Carers' Charter in progress will be further developed by the new European network organisation EUROCARERS in order to stimulate further activities both on national and European policy levels.

To promote wider and continuous transfer and dissemination, EUROFAM-CARE reports and results will be published in a series called "Supporting Family Carers of Older People in Europe – Empirical Evidence, Policy Trends and Future Perspectives". The Pan-European Background Report is the first publication of the series. The National Background Reports from different European countries – the basis of the Pan-European Background Report – will follow this publication.

We hope this will help to raise the recognition of all those who are caring for their elderly family members.

Hamburg in October 2005

Hanneli Döhner and Christopher Kofahl

The EUROFAMCARE Network

The Members of the EUROFAMCARE Consortium

- **Germany, Hamburg**: University Hospital Hamburg-Eppendorf, Centre of Psychosocial Medicine, Social Gerontology, University of Hamburg (Co-ordination centre) – Hanneli Döhner (Co-ordinator), Christopher Kofahl, Susanne Kohler, Daniel Lüdecke, Eva Mnich, Nadine Lange, Kay Seidl, Martha Meyer

- **Germany, Bremen**: Centre for Social Policy Research / Centre for Applied Nursing Research, University of Bremen – Heinz Rothgang, Roland Becker, Andreas Timm

- **Greece**: SEXTANT Group, Social and Economic Research and Consultancy, Department of Health Services Management, National School for Public Health (NSPH), Athen – Elizabeth Mestheneos, Judy Triantafillou, Costis Prouskas, Katerina Mestheneos, Sofia Kontouka

- **Italy**: INRCA Dipartimento Ricerche Gerontologiche, Ancona – Giovanni Lamura, Cristian Balducci, Maria Gabriella Melchiorre, Sabrina Quattrini, Liana Spazzafumo, Francesca Polverini, Andrea Principi, Marie Victoria Gianelli

- **Poland**: Department of Geriatrics, The Medical University of Bialystok; Insitute of Social Economy, Warsaw School of Economics and Institute of Philosophy and Sociology, University of Gdansk – Barbara Bien, Beata Wojszel, Brunon Synak, Piotr Czekanowski, Piotr Bledowski, Wojciech Pedich, Mikolaj Rybaczuk, Bożena Sielawa

- **Sweden**: Department of Health and Society, Linköping University – Birgitta Öberg, Barbro Krevers, Sven Lennarth Johansson, Thomas Davidson

- **United Kingdom**: SISA - Community Sciences Centre and School of Nursing & Midwifery, Northern General Hospital, University of Sheffield – Mike Nolan, Kevin McKee K, Jayne Brown, Louise Barber

- **AGE - The European Older People's Platform**, Brüssel, Belgien – Anne-Sophie Parent, Catherine Daurèle, Jyostna Patel

The members of the Pan-European Group:

- Josef Hörl (Austria)
- Anja Declerq, Chantal Van Audenhove (Belgium)
- Lilia Dimova, Martin Dimov (Bulgaria)
- Iva Holmerová (Czech Republic)
- George W. Leeson (Denmark)

- Terttu Parkatti, Päivi Eskola (Finland)
- Hannelore Jani (France)
- Zsuzsa Széman (Hungary)
- Mary McMahon, Brigid Barron (Ireland)
- Dieter Ferring, Germain Weber (Luxembourg)
- Joseph Troisi (Malta)
- Reidun Ingebretsen, John Eriksen (Norway)
- Liliana Sousa, Daniela Figueiredo (Portugal)
- Simona Hvalic Touzery (Slovenia)
- Arantza Larizgoita Jauregi (Spain)
- Astrid Stückelberger, Philippe Wanner (Switzerland)
- Geraldine Visser-Jansen, Kees Knipscheer (The Netherlands)

The Members of the International Advisory Board

- Robert Anderson, European Foundation for Improvement of Living and Working Conditions, Dublin
- Prof. Dr. Janet Askham, King's College London, Institute of Gerontology, Age Concern, London
- Dr. Stephane Jacobzone, OECD, Social Policy Division, Paris
- Dr. Kai Leichsenring, European Centre for Social Welfare Policy and Research, Wien
- Prof. Dr. Jozef Pacolet, Catholic University of Leuven, Higher Institute of Labour Studies Social and Economic Policy, Leuven
- Marja Pijl, The Netherlands Platform Older People and Europe (NPOE)
- Prof. Dr. Joseph Troisi, University of Malta, Institute of Gerontology
- Prof. Dr. Lis Wagner, WHO - European Office, Kopenhagen

Every partner in the six core countries is also support by a National Advisory Group.

Introduction by the Authors

Many European and national reports have been written about the issue of care for older dependent people.[1] This report is designed to focus on family carers of older people and their situation while later we consider how services do and do not help those who, in virtually every country studied in this report, provide a vast amount of care and support – those termed family and informal carers. It has been designed to be brief, to provide an overview of the 23 countries through their National Background Reports (NABAREs), and to act as a stimulus to all those involved in issues related to care.

The report rests on the expertise of the authors of the national reports and those interested in specific details for each country should examine these reports. Both the final draft of this report and the matrices attached to the report have been circulated between the authors for feedback and final adaptations. The country specific findings and suggestions were re-assessed in the context of the findings from the other NABAREs. We thank all authors for their additional engagement in checking this report in order to improve consistency and reliability.

It is hoped that family carers, policy makers and service providers will find something of interest in this report and that it will provide ideas about how best to move forward in supporting both family carers and older dependent people. At the EU level, the family care of dependent older people is being increasingly recognised as a significant issue, related as it is to the three keystones of accessibility, quality and sustainability of health care systems, to social inclusion and work (labour market).

Elizabeth Mestheneos and Judy Triantafillou

---

[1] Related studies and programmes include CARMEN, FELICIE, IPROSEC, OASIS, PROCARE, SHARE, SOCCARE, European Observatory on the Family, European Foundation studies and reports from these and WHO reports. See References.

1 Background to the Report

1.1 The EUROFAMCARE Study

In all EU countries, the responsibility for the provision of and payment for long-term care is divided between the four sectors of what has been termed the "welfare diamond" (Pijl 1994), namely:

■ Family and informal care sector

■ State or public sector

■ Voluntary and non-governmental-organisation (NGO) sector

■ Care market or private sector

The balance of care provision in each country depends on a mixture of factors such as tradition, legal responsibilities, health and social policy, national budgets and national wealth and, last but not least, demographic trends regarding fertility levels and life expectancy, which affect the availability of informal family carers.

There are substantive differences between countries in Europe as to how care is provided. Those with poorly funded welfare states and a continuing association between poverty and old age, such as Greece and Spain, are associated with low service provision limited to those who can pay or who lack alternative sources of care, whereas in those countries with very high taxation, such as Denmark, demand for services as a taxpayer's right is high. However since demand is potentially infinite, even countries which provide services as a citizen's right inevitably have to introduce a system of rationing, usually based on needs assessment (objective assessment of need for a service) and means testing (income and assets assessment of the older people and / or family carers) to ascertain the older person's ability to make a financial contribution to payment for care. The former Communist regimes with their previous welfare infrastructures are gradually being reconstructed with a plurality of partners from state, local authority, NGO and private sectors.

Despite wide variations in systems of formal care provision for dependent older people, in all the 23 EUROFAMCARE countries the vast majority of care is provided by individual family members within the informal care sector. In countries such as Sweden, where the state has traditionally been a main provider of care, the need to contain increasing costs[2], in combination with the stated preferences of older people themselves to remain in their home environment for as long as possible, has led to what has been described as a "rediscovery of family care" (Johansson 2004). This involves various measures to

---

[2] With a total tax pressure at 50% Swedes expect comprehensive care services and meeting additional caring costs by increasing income tax further would not appear to be a political option.

promote and support the increased participation of the informal care sector via the public and voluntary / NGO sectors[3].

The EUROFAMCARE study focuses on this major contribution of family carers of older dependent people in Europe to the overall provision of long-term care, by compiling comparative data on the situation of family carers through:

- National Background Reports (NABAREs) describing the current situation of family carers in 23 EU countries (AT, BE, BU, CH, CZ, DE, DK, EL, ES, FI, FR, HU, IE, IT, LU, MT, NL, NO, PL, PT, SE, SI, UK). http://www.uke.uni-hamburg.de/extern/eurofamcare/presentations.html

- A Pan-European Background Report (PEUBARE) based on the NABAREs and covering national and European policies and their implications

- National Surveys (NASURs) providing primary data on the experiences of family carers and service use, collected during interviews with 1000 family carers in each of the six core countries (DE, EL, IT, PL, SE, UK)

- A Trans-European Survey Report (TEUSURE)

- A Socio-economic Evaluation (ECO) and a European Policy Analysis

- Research Action (REACT), the final phase of the study, consisting of activities at the local, national and EU level, which aim to improve the situation of family carers

The aim of the NABARES was to collect systematic and comparable data on the situation of family carers in each country, based on a Standardized Evaluation Protocol – STEP (Annex 3), to facilitate the comparative analysis to be used for the production of this Pan-European Background Report. As a corollary to the STEP for the NABARES, the authors were asked to write three overviews with key points to be used for national and EU policy recommendations in the final phase of the project and aimed at:

- Representative organisations of family carers and older people

- Service providers

- Policy makers

1.2   Data Analysis

Despite the use of a detailed Standardized Evaluation Protocol, the main problem in analyzing the NABARES was both the lack of data on family carers from many countries and the wide variation in how available data were recorded, leading to non-comparability of findings between countries. Despite these diffi-

---

[3]   The voluntary/NGO sector in many European countries contracts with the public sector to organise and provide services, thus acting essentially as an enterprise. This is distinct from the work of informal, non paid volunteers.

culties, the authors have selected and focused on key aspects relating to care for dependent older people and some of the key issues which recurred in most reports and have tried to draw some conclusions on the present state of family care in those 23 countries, with a view to making recommendations for future policy for the support of family carers at both national and EU levels.

Family carers currently provide the vast majority of care for dependent older people in all the countries studied, with strong indications that they will continue to do so in the foreseeable future. Thus, one of the main themes of the report are the different methods of support for family carers to give them choices in what aspects of care they provide, to enable them to provide care without damage to their own physical, mental and social well-being and to avoid long term poverty.

The short and long term outcomes and impact of the different types of support for the well-being of older people and family carers, as well as for national and EU economies, are also referred to, although these issues are examined in depth in the socio-economic and policy reports.[4]

1.3 Analytic Matrices

Using the data from the 23 reports, 8 matrices were developed as a way of analysing the large amount of data; these have been used as the basis for the report. The matrices include:

- Legal position of family carers and recognition by the state

- Labour force, informal and formal

- Home-based services for older people

- Services for the support of family carers

- Residential care

- Other issues

- Current policy debates

- Recommendations and future research needs

6 of these matrices are found in Annex 1, the matrix "future research needs" is in Annex 2, whereas "current policy debates" and "recommendations" have been incorporated into the text in sections 2.7 and 3 of the report.

---

[4]　ECO and the Social Policy Report

Throughout the text, stars indicate brief descriptions of interesting, innovative or good practice. It should be noted that these simply provide examples from each country and are not meant to be an extensive and complete list. Full details of good practices can be found in the National Background Reports referred to and available on: http://www.uke.uni-hamburg.de/extern/eurofamcare/ presentations.html

1.4   What is Family Care?

The relations between people are based on social reciprocity, often reflected in legal contracts, and including obligations set up between people, typically kin, over a life time. Family carers of all kinds and of all ages, grow up with their society's social norms and obligations. They also belong within a larger value and ideological system of political and religious belief – capitalism and free market systems, socialism, communism, Catholicism, Protestantism and Orthodoxy, Judaism, Islam- which enshrine in certain dogma the values attached to care for one another, the role of the family and of women. The historic change in Europe has been towards the development of societies and economies that offer people far more choices regarding the kinds of relationships they will set up (Giddens 1991).

Defining the nature of family care for older people who need a range of help with the activities of daily life and financial support is a complex one. Shared histories, love and mutual obligations are at the heart of an interpersonal social solidarity that provides both emotional and practical support between family members. The difficulties arise when the older person's needs become such that they require help over and beyond these 'normal' interchanges. The sudden onset of dependency following, for example, a stroke, requires an immediate response of increased support from both formal and informal care providers. However, when dependency develops more gradually individuals tend to hardly notice the slowly increasing need for help. This is particularly the case for spouses where mutual dependency is often a well developed life strategy. The reports from the 23 countries indicate highly variable rates of spouse care which cannot easily be explained by marriage rates, the relative survival rates of men and women or patterns of co-residence. In countries providing directly comparable data it was reported that in Spain 12.4 % of family carers were spouse carers, in the Netherlands 14 %, in the UK 16 %, 21 % in the Czech Republic, 29.2 % in Poland, while in Finland 43 % were spouse carers. In trying to explain such large differences in reported rates of spouse care, the way in which the research was conducted plays an undoubtedly significant role, depending both on the definition of care used and also on whether the person interviewed was the older person or child or spouse carer. Thus a spouse carer might see himself or herself as being the main carer, while their child might also respond that they provide a lot of care. Hence, comparing percentages of spouse carers or data on child carers does not necessarily indicate significant differences in practice.

This is a necessary preamble to reading this report since the point at which individuals providing care, or the authorities that offer professional care, define an individual as being in a caring role vary substantially. For each individual the point at which they recognize that they are a family carer varies. The man who can no longer count on his wife being able to cook safely, may find this the point at which care becomes a burden; while a child may find dealing with a parent's failing memory the point of irritation and burden.

What is family care? From the outset of the EUROFAMCARE study its clear definition was essential since it had direct implications for selecting the sample of family carers for the 6 national surveys. Thus, although the UK is unique in having a legal definition of who is a family carer which is supported by 3 Acts of Parliament, in the context of this study family care was defined as

"Care and / or financial support provided by a family member for a person 65 years of age or over needing at least 4 hours of personal care or support per week, at home or in a residential care institution."

However, given the massive social changes in terms of work, the role of women, the size of families, the more frequent occurrence of non-marital partnerships with unclear social and legal obligations, divorce and the reformation of families, the growth of single person households and the varying role of friends and neighbours, it is not surprising that the portrait of the 'typical' family carer emerging from discussions amongst the partners was as varied as people themselves.

Nonetheless, certain trends in family care might be expected, in line with more general socio-economic changes such as towards a more urban, educated population and to greater economic resources, even if older people themselves may not always take the largest share in this. Other factors likely to affect family care are better housing and home conditions, social and technological changes that already make home and personal care easier (e.g. ready made meals, home delivery, washing machines, telephones, central heating etc.) and the potential for new technologies to make even greater contributions to home care in the near future (smart homes, robotics, telemedicine). These socio-economic changes have occurred and are occurring at quite different rates in the various countries.

2 Key Issues

2.1 Demographic Trends

Who precisely provides family care varies substantially, relating in part to demographic developments that have occurred in each country. Demographic trends, including declining birth rates and increasing life expectancy, have occurred throughout the 23 countries. However, the exact time at which the birth rates declined in each country vary, with Hungary being one country that experienced a low birth rate several decades ago and Ireland being a country with a relatively recent decline. This aspect of demographic change should not be ignored since it provides an understanding of the 'stock' of kin and family members available to care in the population both currently and in the future. Other demographic changes that have occurred also have a substantive impact on the availability of family carers. These include the decline in marriage rates, the rise in divorce rates (excluding Poland), the decline in the size of households and the increase in single person households and patterns of rural-urban and international migration. Each of these factors, in addition to poverty rates and the distribution of income between the generations and age groups, occurs with variations between the 23 countries *(2003 The Social Situation in the European Union.* European Commission. Eurostat).

 Belgium has taken the demographic projections seriously and, recognizing the baby boom and subsequent low birth rate, set up a Silver Fund to meet the needs for pensions and care as consequences of the ageing population after 2030.

2.2 Legal Obligations and Family Care and the Role of the State

The legal situation regarding care obligations within the family varied widely amongst the 23 NABARES countries, as did the enforceability of the law. Given that the law represents an enshrinement of specific social attitudes and expectations and is constantly being modified, it was considered important to review the very different situation of family carers in the 23 countries, regarding both responsibilities and rights.

Legal obligations to care consist of financial responsibilities and duties to provide practical "care", although the two cannot always be clearly distinguished.

Moreover, legal obligations to care are different for spouses and children

■ Spouses have ethical and legal obligations to mutual support and care

■ Children's obligations are not as clearly defined as those of spouses, if at all.

However, changing social patterns across Europe, with the increase of "partner" relationships particularly in Northern Europe without the legal ties of marriage, may lead to different care obligations between partners, as well as partners' children, and the increase in divorce and re-marriage is creating new family networks with an associated lack of clarity regarding obligations and willingness to care.

Legal enforcement of family care duties

The enforceability of laws regarding family obligations to support dependent members, depended on the type of support specified, although almost no country could cite any case law examples where the practical duties of families to care were legally enforced. Portugal was the country that considered case law existed for the enforcement of care by families, while in Poland there were joint legal inheritance agreements on inheritance in exchange for care. Spain also cited that infringement to fulfil legal duties to assist could be punished with arrest from eight to twenty weekends under the Spanish Penal Code, though how often this was enforced in practice was not clear.

However, legal enforcement of financial support by children for their dependent parents was reported by many countries with regard to family contribution to payments for care (AT, BE, FR, DE, IE (recently repealed), IT, NL, PL, ES, PT, SI, UK). This is achieved by:

■ "Means testing" of the dependent older person and / or spouse and / or children to pre-determine their financial ability to contribute to the costs of care, e.g. in the UK, an older person must contribute to the costs of care if they have assets above a certain level.

■ Reclaiming costs of care via means testing of children's "inheritance", e.g. in France, the state is legally entitled to deduct the costs of residential care from the dependent older person's estate on death

In both cases the family's financial participation in the costs of care, if they are able to, is ensured. The practical provision of care by family carers, however, appears to be legally non-enforceable and, though spouse care would seem to be part of the marriage contract, care by children and kin is essentially voluntary.

In summary, amongst the 23 countries, **primary legal responsibility** for the *care of dependent older people* was as follows:

1. Spouse care obligation specified, financial and / or care (AT, FR, HU-until the change in regime, ES)

2. Child care obligation specified, financial and / or care (AT, BE, BU, FR, DE, EL, IT, MT, PL, ES, PT, SI)

3. State / local authority (CZ, DK, FI, LU, NL, NO, SE, UK)

4. Unclear or variable legal rights (IE, CH, HU)

In 1 and 2, the state assumes responsibility only if the family is unable i.e. there is an obligation on the part of the older person to show evidence of the family's inability to care, such as no family members available, financial or social difficulties etc. There is no state obligation or incentive to provide needs assessment, but the older person and the family may be means tested to assess eligibility for service.

In 3, the state, whether at national, regional or local level, assumes primary responsibility, using varied systems to encourage or support family carers in sharing care. This implies that services are provided according to need (needs assessment), with or without a financial contribution (the older person and / or family are means tested).

2.3 The Role of Family Care and Social Attitudes

Attitudes towards family care vary throughout Europe, but also within the individual countries, e.g. urban / rural, middle / working class. Although an attempt has been made to classify these variations in attitudes towards family care, there is really a spectrum which is often also related to levels of formal service provision for the older person.

- High social expectations to provide care, no formal recognition
  FR, EL, HU, PL, ES, PT

- High social expectations to provide care, increasing formal recognition
  AT, DE ambivalent, IE, IT, MT, NL

- Low social expectations about family care, no formal recognition
  BU, CZ, DK, LU, SI, CH

- Low social expectations, increasing formal recognition
  BE, FI, NO, SE, UK.

At the individual country levels however, wide variations in the approaches to family care exist, exemplified even within the Scandinavian countries with their traditionally high levels of health and social care services.

The **Danish** approach is to focus on the continuation and expansion of services to meet the increasing demands of an ageing population, with little recognition of the role that informal family care does or could play in future planning. This approach reflects the similar policy for care of children, where high levels of female labour market participation are supported by high provision of public infant and child care services.

Sweden in contrast, despite similarly high levels of women working outside the home and of service provision for older people, is experiencing a "rediscovery" of family care and has recognised the value of and need to support family carers, in combination with good and adequate services.

Many countries would envy the efficiency of Sweden where the development and implementation of a 3 Year Action Plan (1999-2001) stimulated Local Authorities to develop an infrastructure of services targeting family caregivers, e.g. by setting up caregiver resource centres offering training, counselling, support groups, respite care, in-formation and resources for family caregivers, including day care programs for their disabled family members.

Interestingly, in **Norway,** where very detailed information is available from specific projects on who undertakes different caring tasks for the support of dependent older people, women in paid work are reported to provide more in-formal care than non-working women. Nevertheless, the role of the Norwegian family carer is considered to have a supervisory nature rather than providing regular "hands on" care, due to high levels of service provision, although the Action Plan for the Elderly specifically underlines "the importance of taking care of and supporting the caregiving ability of families."

In **Finland** a significant part of daily activities (cleaning, shopping, laundry etc.) for older people living at home, including the very dependent, is undertaken by relatives either with or without public support. Without family carers there would be a lot more pressure for institutional care and there are indications that older people would like to give more responsibility to relatives for their care. The importance of family caregiving has been noted in Finnish society by policy makers.

The administrator appointed by the Finnish Ministry of Social Af-fairs and Health, recently (March 2004) made a proposal contain-ing 16 recommendations involving family carers' well-being, pay and leisure as a way of developing the status of carers as part of social and health services. The aim is to give the family caregiver the status of a municipal worker, with these changes being intro-duced gradually and completed by 2012. Services are mainly pub-lic with the municipalities contracting to private agencies to fill the gap between demand and supply.

In summary, the "Scandinavian model" of care, based on a high level of ser-vice provision, in fact displays 4 different examples or models of care for older people when viewed from the perspective of the family carer.

A quite different model is being developed in the UK, Ireland and the Nether-lands where family carers are being recognised as a group of citizens with special rights.

The UK is unique in giving legal recognition and associated rights and services to family carers, enshrined in the Carers' (Equal Opportunities) Act 2004.

At the other end of Europe, the "southern European" or "family model" of care, exemplified in EUROFAMCARE by Portugal, Malta, Greece, Italy and Spain, also displays broad differences in developing services and support for older people and their family carers in response to demographic and social changes. Traditionally, **Portugal** has many women in the paid labour market and as a result makes more use of residential and home care services for very dependent elderly people; this contrasts with **Greece** with a low labour market participation rate of women, a low use of residential and home care services and a turn to using migrant care workers by those who can afford it.

2.4 The "Work" of Caring

2.4.1 Family Carers

Family carers were rarely considered in the 23 countries as part of the paid labour force, with the main focus of interest and data being on the potential and actual impact of family care on labour market participation. Nonetheless family carers do provide their labour, mostly unpaid, to support the dependent older person; the supply, availability and willingness of individuals to act as family carers is critical in understanding the long term trends in labour provision for care work. The difficulty revolves around the unpaid and unrecognized nature of domestic work – a problem faced by economists and statisticians. Is family care and domestic maintenance part of the national economy or not? Where this work is undertaken by paid persons it is counted as falling within the labour force, though not when unregistered.

 As might be expected, the Swiss have studied the economic value of family care work, which they calculated to reach between 10 and 12 billions of Swiss Francs, exceeding the cumulative spending on both home care services and residential care homes.

Thus the rate of women's participation, or non participation, in the labour market is often a dimension of labour availability for care work. The critical issue in the labour market for care work lies in whether the individuals providing domestic and care work are officially paid with national insurance and tax contributions or not. The debate also revolves around the 'work' people do to support one another, as part of normal social exchanges, and that which goes beyond these 'normal' interchanges to become defined as 'work'. Only a few countries have provided any estimate of the total amount of time and thus 'work' provided by family carers – Norway reports that care for those over 67 years of age takes approximately 49,000 man years per annum. Yet this involves all kinds of care and rarely in the national reports or literature is sufficient distinction made between 'normal' care and support, and the labour involved when people become very dependent. Nonetheless data on dependent older people shows that in many countries (AT, BE, IT, CZ), 70-80 % of care was given by family carers. This contrasts with data from Denmark that shows that less than 55 % of older people get family care support.

Data from national studies on the proportion of the population giving care are not very helpful for comparative purposes, since the nature of this care, the size of households or which ages are counted as being potential family carers varies widely, ranging from the whole population to those aged 16 or 18, with variable cut off points, e.g. aged 65 or age 74. An example of this kind of difficulty in comparing data can be seen when examining the data on Portugal where 2.3 % of the population are reported as caring for an older person, Spain, where 5 % of those aged 18+ are reported as providing family care to a dependent older person, equivalent to 12.4 % of households, Switzerland, where 23.1 % of the population are reported as caring for someone aged 65 and over, and the Netherlands, where 18.8 % of the population 18+ (2 million) report caring for someone 64 years and above. Some of these differences in rates of family care between countries are frankly counter-intuitive.

The national reports provide indications that even within countries there are often massive variations in the amount of family care provided; UK, Ireland, Italy and Spain report such significant variations, e.g. more in the South than the North of Italy, and more in Northern England than London, while other counties report large urban-rural differences. Thus the difficulty does not lie in the accuracy of national data per se but the lack of comparability in studies and the criteria used to measure family care.

2.4.2 Characteristics of Family Carers

Given some of the specified problems in defining family carers, what does emerge in many reports is the **predominance of women**, whether as child, sister, spouse or friend / neighbour carers. Though the rates vary, overall approximately two thirds of care[5] is provided by women. However, where data are available for care for the most dependent, the numbers of women carers rises, e.g. in Italy, the proportion rises from 66 % to 81 % for heavy care, while for those receiving allowances, normally awarded for the care of the most heavily dependent, the figures from Luxembourg and Spain show figures of 94.2 % and 83 % women respectively. In Germany, amongst the terminally ill 81 % of family carers were female: wives, daughters or daughters in law.

---

[5]   66.33% BE; 64% CZ; 75% FI; 75% PT: 69-74% MT; Women give 2.5 x more care than men NO.

Amongst these, 32 % were also in paid employment with the proportion for daughters being 61 %; 87 % of them additionally were responsible for their own household. This kind of pressure on women inevitably had repercussions on their own mental and physical health and this is discussed later.

Yet where care is provided by older people to each other, then there is a greater gender balance: Poland and Switzerland reported equal proportions of male family carers in the 50+ age groups while the UK reported no gender differences in family care for co-resident carers, though women do more care in another household in both Switzerland and the UK. In Italy, 10 % of family care was provided by people who were themselves over 80 years of age.

Although in many countries children, especially daughters and daughters in law provide a large percentage of family care, e.g. nearly 75 % were child carers in Malta, there were large variations. In Hungary, daughters constituted 11.3 % and sons 8.7 % of all family carers compared to 37.1 % daughters and 20.9 % sons and 15.5 % grandchildren in Poland.

Social changes in marital and family relationships in Europe are often assumed to have implications for the availability of family carers. In the case of spouse versus other forms of non legal partnership, the data from the national reports was not clear; thus no valid reflections can be made on this issue in this report. Demographic differences between countries may account for some of the variation in who cared; sibling care, especially by sisters, was pointed out to be important in Slovenia. However, in examining the variations in who provided care in a range of countries where data are available, the role of the wider family, neighbours and friends, was evident. In Spain, relatives other than parents, spouses and in laws provided 14 % of care, while neighbours and caretakers provide 5.6 % and friends 4 %; in Hungary in rural areas 19.2 % of older people relied on friends and 34.4 % on neighbours; in the Czech Republic 16 % relied on friends and 10 % on other relatives while in Belgium the wider family cared for 17 % of dependent older people needing care while non-family carers were responsible for 13.3 % of care.

The age of the carer, the current state of the labour market and women's participation in the labour market all appeared to have a direct influence on those who both worked and cared. There were a number of countries marked by the high rates of labour market participation (80 %) for women until the age of 55 years, including CZ, DK, PT, SE and FI. This was reflected in the fact that a large proportion of carers were employed; however, again one should be careful as the degree of dependency of those they cared for was often less than in other countries. Thus in Portugal at a certain level of dependency it appeared that older people went into residential care, while in Sweden and the Czech Republic there were a variety of forms of residential support for those who could no longer easily be cared for at home. As suggested, the percentage of those using any and all forms of residential care has to be considered in order to understand the ability of family carers to hold down full time jobs. In addition, the hours given to care must be carefully examined, with the suggestion that working carers probably give fewer hours to care. This compares with figures for Spain where 22 % of family carers were employed (36 % part time and 64 % full time), or Poland where a third worked and cared.

In several countries family carers were reported as being more likely to be housewives, pensioners or unemployed (BE, EL, DE, ES). Germany reported that civil servants, the self employed and the salaried were those in the labour market who were most likely to combine work with care, though overall those caring for older people without dementia were more engaged in the labour market (30.9 %) than those caring for a person with dementia (25.3 %). In Switzerland, 33 % of the self employed provided care, while 21.8 % of the unemployed did so. Ireland brought some interesting data to show that despite the huge increase in labour participation rates for women (50 %), they continued to do the same amount of caring as the non-employed. Such data suggests again the difficulties of unravelling the concept of care. Those who work may be far more inclined to notice that they are also caring than those who do not work. The decline in rates of employment for women, especially in the Eastern European countries, has implications as to the availability of people to care, e.g. in Slovenia, though also in France. Yet internal and external migration, e.g. in Bulgaria, Hungary, and Greece may leave many older people with fewer available carers.

The economic aspects of family care are also reflected indirectly in the information from Austria that amongst the 40 % who were employed and cared, those with low status jobs were more likely to undertake work and hands on care. In Italy, family carers tended to have more available income than non-caring households yet 60 % were unhappy with their economic situation; these data probably reflect the pooling of resources by the family carer and older person in a common budget.

There are often considerable details on the average age of carers – yet as already indicated the (self-) definition of family care makes such data problematic in a cross country review.

The trends observed by national experts are important in deciding on the future availability of family carers, all other matters being constant[6]. Several countries perceived a trend in the decline in willingness to provide hands on care especially amongst the better educated and those with better jobs (AT, DE, NO) and this was also noticeable among women, where the large increase in the numbers working and / or the availability of long-term care insurance (LCI) allowed many to retreat from care (FI, IE, DE, MT, NL). Belgium noted the increased mobility in society, making family care less available, while Hungary and Malta noted the trend that older people and family carers

---

[6]   Of course they are not constant. Thus in Sweden the decision to support family carers may increase the numbers of people offering care to dependent older people.

less often share a common household. A number of countries commented on the increase in the numbers of male carers (HU, EL, IE, IT, MT, SE) and Norway and Sweden noted that the total amount of family care has increased though the hours spent has decreased, which is in line with the provision of more care services. Finally, some authors commented on the changes in attitudes amongst older people; some perceived their families as less willing to care (BE) and others, including the Netherlands, suggested that there was evidence that the better educated preferred public and private services rather than help and care from their kin.

2.4.3 Is Family Care 'real' Work?

Studies from various countries provide some perspective on the number of hours for which family carers worked to support dependent older people. In Portugal, 68.3 % of family carers provided more that 4 hours per day and 56.6 % provided care every day. In Ireland, the breakdown of hours provided by family carers showed that 60.3 % worked 1-19 hrs, 13.4 % - 30-49 hrs and 26.7 % more than 50 hrs per week. Luxembourg, which provided a detailed breakdown for the hours of care given to dependent people of all ages indicated that the young disabled needed most care followed by the oldest age group (90+) and that overall 35 % of dependent people needed in excess of 24 hours per week. In the Netherlands, the average amount of care amounted to 17.9 hours per week, including domestic help, psychosocial support and personal care. These indicative numbers suggest that taking on the care of someone means for many people to invest a lot of their time and perhaps a half of all carers have, effectively, the equivalent of a half time 'job'. For the most dependent, including, for example, those with dementia or those at the very end of life, the hours needing to be spent in care rise substantially. Unlike the care of children, family care of dependent older people cannot be programmed precisely. The gradual nature of increasing dependence is the usual scenario, though not even this is predictable and age related decline in functional ability may include significant periods of decreased or increased dependency (Robine, Romieu, 1998). The lack of ability to 'programme' the work needed is one of the characteristic problems of family care work with older people and, indeed, care from service providers[7].

Another aspect that reflects on the nature of the work of a family carer is the issue of its consequences to their health and well being. As already discussed, the levels and types of care provided in countries varies, but given that in many only inadequate services to support both older people and their family carers exist, what does emerge widely from the reports is that the provision of care has both physical and mental consequences. France reported that family carers had double the risk of depression than in the general population, a finding that is supported in other countries where depression and psychological

---

[7] Hence the interest in discussions on the cultural as well as the health aspects of dependency.

burden were noted as being very frequent. In Portugal, where depression was also an issue among family carers, the report also indicated that needs and problems vary by income levels, with leisure being more of an issue for the better off and financial help for the worse off.

Also commonly more frequently reported amongst family carers than for the general population were physical problems that were consequences arising from care. For example, the German report states exhaustion, pain in arms and legs, bad backs, heart trouble and severe stomach pain. These symptoms were more pronounced amongst those caring for the cognitively impaired. Social isolation and the inability to participate in normal family and social life, mentioned in the Slovenia report, is undoubtedly a widespread phenomenon. For care-providing ageing spouses, fears of what would happen if they died or could no longer manage, was a specific issue mentioned in the Danish report, but probably a common theme for spouse carers in many countries; the Netherlands noted that spouse carers were less likely to use services, though caring full time, while Norway reported health risks for older people providing long term care for spouses with dementia.

One aspect of family and professional care that helps in understanding the nature of the work and particularly its emotional consequences is that which concerns abuse. Most countries have no or very little data on the issue[8]. Slovenia reported research that found a staggering 50 % of older people were abused by their children, with family members or relatives being responsible for three quarters of incidences of abuse and the explanation being found in the exhaustion of family carers, although 10.9 % were also abused in the institutions where they lived. The Scandinavian countries provide figures for elderly abuse that vary from 1 % to 8 %, with abuse more common in urban areas. In one study in Germany, 10.8 % of older people, disproportionately older women, reported violence against them, though psychological maltreatment and financial abuse were more frequent. In the Italian report, reference was made to recent research monitoring 2,500 people aged over 60 in a number of European countries; Italian older people were those reporting most loneliness and neglect for which they held their children responsible[9]. Domestic violence is generally hidden.

A study in the UK indicated one in three old people were psychologically abused; one in five physically abused and the same number has their savings inappropriately used; more than 10 % are neglected and 2.4 % sexually abused. There is also only limited data on abuse of older people in residential care.

---

[8] In addition, data is often not comparable since the research definitions used vary.
[9] Like dependency, this is often a matter of cultural and individual definition.

In Italy pioneering projects in Turin, Rome, Milan and Genoa support elderly victims of abuse as collaborative ventures between municipal authorities and local voluntary agencies.

Germany and Italy point to the fact that there is also inadequate data on abuse by older people against their family carers.

What is important to underline is that interpersonal relations may become very tested when dependency becomes a characteristic within the relationship. Interventions in such situations require a well developed and proactive psychological service and it may be more effective to provide more respite care than to try to alter the relationships between the family carer and older person.

 The Czech Alzheimer Society started a new project, "granny sitting", that provides family caregivers with regular respite.

In the general framework of training for all carers, the issue of dealing with anger, frustration and difficult interpersonal relations should also be confronted.

 In Malta, where the Catholic church is important, two church-based organizations give training called "Care for Carers" designed to reduce stressful situations, improve communications, as well as provide care in a more effective and efficient manner.

In discussing the issues of the hard and difficult work of family carers it should not be forgotten that many obtain satisfactions from their caring work; interestingly this aspect rarely emerged in the research quoted in the national reports.[10] The UK was one exception to this; studies which included minority ethnic groups indicated that the extent of care giving satisfactions outnumbered the difficulties with the dynamics of the relationship between care giver and older person being the key factor.

The value arising from the recognition that the work provided by family carers often has real health and social costs for them, lies in considering which services can best relieve and support them, e.g. in confronting depression, in reducing the physical toll and social isolation. Another aspect is that some of the same issues may also arise when considering care work conducted by professionals; learning specific skills and having appropriate practical and psychological support may play significant roles in helping both family and professional carers.

---

[10] This is likely to be the result of consistent value judgements by researchers who focus on burden rather than satisfactions.

In Slovenia, the Anton Trstenjak Institute provides intergenerational communication programmes so that family members are trained to better understand older people. This has several benefits; the quality of life of older family members is improved, everybody is more pleased due to better family relationships and younger generations become familiar with old age, the first step in preparing for their own ageing.

One such form of support that plays a highly variable role in some countries is that of family carer support groups. While some groups are particularly concerned with advocacy for their rights and the conditions under which they work, many are also important in providing psychological and practical support to one another, e.g. the Alzheimer Society or the Federation of Senior Citizens Organisations – BAGSO – in Germany. As discussed below, such groups may be supported and encouraged by national and local governments.

2.4.4 Reciprocity in Family Care Work

Property, savings and life time exchanges between the older person and the family carer have to be taken into account when examining the willingness of individuals to take on care. While not the primary motivation from the perspective of the family carer, it may still play a significant role in the reasons people feel there are obligations to care, though there is limited research on the subject. Research in Norway indicated that despite the fact that there are considerable transfers from older people as inheritance, pre-inheritance and gifts, this did not generally influence the amount of care given to older parents by children. If parents are in need of nursing, previous practical help from parents to children, including child care, resulted in more nursing care by children. Overall older people gave more help and economic support to the younger generations, compared to the help they received. The German report stressed that moral obligations and financial considerations are not mutually exclusive in family care. In three countries, Belgium, Denmark and Finland, property and savings were said to play no part in family care. In Spain, 63 % of family carers indicated that the older person gave them no economic rewards, 23 % regularly received compensation and 13 % occasionally; but the overall costs to the household of providing care were substantial, especially those with a medium-low economic status, since pensions are low and do not even cover the costs of care.

Overall in 15 of the country reports property and economic transfers were stated as playing some role in family care. In Austria, one study showed that 72 % of family carers considered transfers to be important and only 28 % felt that inheritance plays "a negligible role" in inter-generational relations. In Bulgaria, Poland and Italy, inheritance was important and if a family took the older person's property and then did not provide care the state intervened. In three countries, Hungary, Slovenia and Poland, explicit mention was made of the value of the older person's pension to the carers, given the high rates of unemployment. Slovenia, Ireland and UK mentioned that older people often want to be able to pass on their property to their children, leading to reluctance to seek other kinds of care solutions or support which would involve them selling their assets.

With reference to long term trends in willingness to care, it is necessary to consider if such exchanges and inheritance are likely to continue to be important. It may be presumed that where the older person offers a scarce economic resource this aspect will continue to be significant, though much less so where their children have their own resources. One hypothesis might be that older people either with resources or, as the Portuguese and Norwegian reports indicate, who have given a lot of time and energy to the practical support of their children, are more likely to receive care.

2.4.5 Professional Paid Care

In discussing services to support older people and family carers, the availability, training and qualities of all those employed to work in the care sector need to be considered, since they provide the context in which family carers can genuinely rely on support and help in their work. Care work in both residential and home care services is overwhelmingly being provided in the public sector. Nonetheless the growth of organised private sector services was reported in Austria, Finland, Germany, Greece[11] (very limited), Ireland, Italy, Luxembourg, Netherlands, Norway, Poland, UK and Slovenia. While it is probable that these private services are more used by the better off amongst older people and their families, few countries reported large differences between the public and private sectors in terms of their attractiveness to care workers or in terms of their ability to recruit and retain care workers. Of particular interest are those countries that reported **few problems** in recruitment and retention of care workers in either the public or private care sector, e.g. The Netherlands, Bulgaria, France, Luxembourg, Malta, Poland, Portugal. Others, like Belgium, have had a problem and are attempting to improve the supply of nurses and care workers by improving working conditions and pay, while in Denmark similar attempts are being made by improving training and attempting to attract more men into caring jobs with older people. All these positive examples are important since they suggest that there is nothing inevitable about the difficulties reported in so many countries in recruiting and retaining care workers for older people.

What are the main difficulties reported in the national reports? These include low pay in Finland, Austria, Greece Hungary, Ireland, Poland, Portugal, UK (especially unqualified staff); the lack of staff leads to unacceptable shift work

---

[11] Reference here is to organised services rather than the growth of migrant care workers who are not normally organised into a service.

and overtime in Austria, Slovenia and Germany, while Poland believes this is a future problem they will face. The low prestige and tiring nature of working with older people was commented on for the Czech Republic, Germany, Greece, Hungary, Italy, Ireland, Sweden, Switzerland and the UK. The lack of a real career and promotion opportunities was commented on by Ireland. Even in Norway there was a high turnover amongst care workers in the urban areas. The predominance of women in care work was a feature of every country – a characteristic that is nearly always associated with lower pay and prestige. In the Netherlands, professional care workers in residential care have increasingly limited time for every patient, due to budget cuts. Increasingly volunteers and family carers are needed to provide care in residential and nursing homes.

Thus one of the critical issues facing most countries is how to improve the status, conditions of employment and attractiveness of working in the care sector for older people in the many countries where care workers are often undertrained and overworked. This is a difficult issue given the fact that public budgets in most countries tend to be limited, unskilled and semi-skilled labour is often readily available and cheap, while the perception and often the realities of work with older people is that it is depressing and hard. Clearly, as some of the 23 countries have managed to improve the status of care work, there are lessons to be learned about how this may be achieved.

One way forward is **training, in combination with the development of a career structure** for care workers. In turn, this requires that all services introduce **quality standards.**

This may be one arena in which interventions from the EU could be a positive influence, e.g. the promotion of minimum standards in care work and ensuring that some EU funded training schemes are devoted to care work. Several countries noted that in private services care workers were often less trained than in the public services.

In Portugal training the long term unemployed to work with older people in a social support service was developed.

In Hungary, with its long-term low birth rate and fewer children to care, NGOs have been active innovators. The Budapest Centre of the Hungarian Maltese Charity Service linked a two year health and social training to the employment of disadvantaged young girls and boys living in poor family circumstances with emotional and family deprivation. On graduation the young people took jobs in care and nursing for older people where they also functioned as quasi grandchildren. The same NGO has also supported the development of networks of voluntary and neighbourhood carers to cope with age-related disability.

However, caution is required in extrapolating from these suggestions and examples; the French report indicated that unless there are clear advantages in
terms of employment and promotion for those with qualifications, and while
public and private bodies continue to hire the unqualified at similar rates to the
qualified, individuals may perceive no real advantage in gaining qualifications.

The **modernisation of services and institutions** represents an important
way of moving forward in making care work more attractive; thus, introducing
new technologies where possible and training both family carers and professional staff would appear to be a positive step forward. Given the under-
funded nature of many public and private care services this may not always be
feasible, but must be considered as a possible strategy at national level.

Making the **conditions of employment** more attractive is another device to
attract and keep care workers; genuinely flexible forms of employment[12] from
the perspective of the employee may be attractive to some individuals. Sweden reported using increasing numbers of part time workers in both home and
residential settings, reflecting contradictions between stakeholders – what is
good for workers may not be good for older people, e.g. with respect to conti-
nuity of care.

*In Belgium a federal initiative Integrated Services for Home Care
(GDTs) help family carers by organizing multi-disciplinary consul-
tation and by helping them to draw up a realistic care plan that
specifies the tasks of each (formal and informal) carer.*

Another area for possible improvement lies in changing attitudes towards older
people and perhaps of older people towards care workers. The experiences of
possible attitude changes in Austria, Germany and Hungary, where young
men may work in care settings for older people instead of doing military service, would be interesting.

*In Denmark the attempt to make care work more attractive to men
is one strategy that needs to be monitored.*

2.4.6 Migrant and foreign Care Workers, legal and illegal

De facto solutions to the recruitment of care workers for older people are being
found in 13 of the 23 countries (AT, CZ, DE, DK, EL, IT, LU, NO, PL, ES, PT,
CH, UK) by the use of migrant and foreign care workers, as domestic, care or
nursing personnel. As is evident, this solution was being used in a wide range
of countries in terms of both income and welfare systems. There were no data

---

[12] Marrying the interests of services, e.g. the need to organise shift work and 24 hour coverage, can
be done in conjunction with the wishes of employees for flexible and/or part-time employment.

for France, but migrant workers were apparently important and for Ireland migrant workers were important in the nursing sector. Belgium and Sweden provided no data. The countries reporting that migrant labour was not important in care work were FI, BU, MT, NL and SI, and only a few reported that foreign born people were less likely to be employed in health and social services; The Netherlands pointed out that a significant impediment for entering this part of the labour market is the requirement for higher education and the poor command of the Dutch language. Recently, in the Western, urbanised part of the Netherlands more migrants are working in the lower care jobs.

One of the difficulties associated with migrant care workers is that though many may be more educated than local care workers, they are rarely trained in care work per se and may have language problems. Many governments, simply by not developing public services and by not having active policies towards the recruitment and legalisation of foreign migrant care workers, are conniving with the current situation which leads to exploitation and a lack of control[13]. Ensuring their legalisation, training (including language), and their incorporation, where feasible, into a caring career, is likely to be important for the coming years until attitudes and practices change substantively in many of the countries reviewed.

2.4.7 The Voluntary Sector

A large number of countries had and have sought to develop volunteer services to help with the care of older people and indirectly for family carers. Austria, France, Belgium, Bulgaria, Hungary, Ireland, Finland (1 % of all care), Germany, Greece, Italy, Malta, Netherlands, Poland, Slovenia, and the UK all reported that volunteers were important in caring for older people, while Sweden and Norway specifically mentioned the importance of volunteers but not for hands on care. One outstanding example is Hungary, where 70,000 NGOs have developed in the past years, 13 % being in the health and care fields. Here volunteers work at lower wages than employees but undertake hands on care. This contrasts with the situation in most countries where volunteers do not undertake a lot of hands on care, but provide important auxiliary services such as transport, accompaniment, social support etc. In a number of countries, family carers' self help groups are also important in terms of offering practical care support.

---

[13] It may well be argued that the private solutions adopted by the middle and upper classes by employing migrant care workers contributes to the lack of political concern with the general situation of family carers.

In Germany the Department for Social Work in Wiesbaden (Hessen) runs a course qualifying people as "voluntary senior citizens' companions" designed to lessen the burden of care and give support to family carers in need of a few hours of free time.

 In the Netherlands the national organisation for Voluntary Palliative and Terminal Care (VPTZ) with 180 local VPTZ-organisations has a well-developed training course for volunteers who are providing palliative and terminal care at home and in hospices to relieve family carers.

In contrast, volunteers played a very limited role in both Spain (0.1 % in care for older people) and Portugal. No data from national reports indicated whether organized volunteering substantially relieved family carers, although in Ireland, 12.5 % of all volunteers provide services for the sick and older people.

2.4.8 The Future of Care Work

The above analysis suggests that the care of older people will continue in many countries to rely heavily on family carers, supported by professional care workers and this is probably in line with the wishes of some family carers who want to care. The overwhelming majority of public budgets can currently not bear the full costs of developing a system of comprehensive care for older people through publicly provided services, especially since future predictions indicate that the demand for care is likely to increase. Thus ensuring that family carers are supported by professional care workers is critical, as are policies and practices that compensate family carers for care undertaken by ensuring that they retain a good quality of life and security in their own retirement. Both these aspects are critical elements to be addressed in policies for family carers.

 In Ireland the development, promotion and adoption of the Carer's Charter marks an attempt to recognise publicly the work and the rights of family carers.

Family carers' recognition can be further promoted through the development of training and changes in attitudes that will ensure that all care workers learn to perceive family carers as vital members of the care staff, with rights to leave, respite care, advice, information and training.

The German Federation of Advice Centres for Older People and Family Carers (BAGA) published a manual for professionals on how to give advice and support to family carers of older people suffering from dementia, including practical training, support groups for older people suffering from dementia, advice and counselling in domestic care environment, volunteer services, café for family carers and Alzheimer-dancing-café sessions. The reader also contains comprehensive information on family caring and relevant legislation.

The systematic training of family carers could be another important development, particularly in creating professional attitudes towards care work and ensuring good standards amongst family carers and safeguards for their own health and well being, although their parallel need for adequate support services in the provision of care should also be emphasized.

In the Spanish autonomous province of the Canary Islands, the "Programme for the Elderly at Risk" includes support to carers offering training activities to 100 % of carers and community support plans for self-help groups and associations.

Such training may also provide a future supply of care workers who after qualification may wish to work in this sector. Another important resource, not fully explored in most countries is the use of more part time care workers in both home and residential care settings.

A further development in the coming years will be the increasing numbers of older people from ethnic minority backgrounds. A number of countries have already developed services for them and some have also recognised the needs of migrant caregivers.

In Germany, concern with migrant family carers is evident in a number of courses being run throughout the country, e.g. a caregiving course in Wiesbaden is offered to Turkish migrants in Turkish and German.

2.4.9 New Technologies

New technological advances have neither been fully developed nor had yet an extensive impact in supporting care work with older people. This is partly due to the low levels of computer literacy amongst many older people, including family carers, and partly due to the difficulties of using new technologies in old homes. The 'smart' house is still a number of years from real implementation, though in countries like the Netherlands alarm systems and ICT-technology are becoming standard equipment. The Italian report indicated that those who could afford it were paying for expensive new technologies including security alarm systems, video-telephones, mechanized shutter locks, tele-medicine devices, mechanised doors / window openers, data networks (for rapid shared access to the Internet), bedroom intercom, visual and auditory signals, remote control apparatus of certain functions via phone. A number of countries including Finland, Germany and the UK are working to develop gerotechnology, e.g. locomotion devices in / out of house, assistive technologies for eating and other activities of daily life, security, e.g. timers for lights, locomotion recognition, security telephone, doorbell alarm, night alarms that wake the family carer if the older person moves from their bed in the night etc. Many countries are seeing the introduction of information and counselling systems designed to be used by family carers and professionals, whether run by local authorities, NGOs or family support groups.

In Sweden a telematics intervention programme (ACTION) has been developed to support family caregivers of older people. The service consists of educational caring programmes, video phone facilities for on-line communication with other carers and a call centre staffed with professionals an access to the Internet. The ACTION service has so far covered 40 families who are very satisfied with this type of support. (Magnusson 2005)

However, cheap and effective solutions such as the Hungarian alarm system between the older person's house and a neighbour are probably the closest many older people and family carers currently get to using and accessing 'new' technologies!

Public investment in all forms of gerotechnology is important for the work of family care and the support of dependent older people[14]. However changes in mainstream developments can also have important implications for family carers. Thus, as both the Greek and French reports point out, cheap mobile phones allow family carers to be in constant communication with the older dependent person. Market penetration of most new technologies aiding family carers will initially be limited in many of the 23 countries due to low incomes. As in all innovations there are both benefits and potential abuses in the use of IT in care work, e.g. the ethical dilemma of constant observation.

2.5 Public Investment in Care and Family Care of Older People

2.5.1 The Right to receive Care

The right to receive care in times of illness, either short or long-term, is now agreed to be a fundamental right within the EU, enshrined and reflected in national laws and the EU Social Charter. Whilst the 23 NABARES countries all

---

[14] The EU is supporting a number of R&D initiatives that may help with care work e.g. smart toilets.

provided a basic health care system at the hospital and primary care levels much wider variations in the provision of **social care services** to older people exist, particularly in regard to home care services and whether these were provided as a statutory right, depending on need (degree of dependency) and financial situation (means tested). The increasing demand by ageing populations in Europe for long-term care for chronic conditions causing disability and dependency emerges as one of the major trends examined in the NABARES reports, with focus on the main issues of who provides care, where is it provided and how is it funded. There are significant inequalities and fragmentation in care provision as long-term care may be provided by either health or social service sectors or both. All 23 countries undertook some responsibility for the care of dependent older people, although there was great variation in:

- The degree of public responsibility
  - Limited, e.g. only for the most disabled, those without financial means, and without family support
  - According to need
- The type of public support available
  - Financial support to the older person or the family carer
  - Services to the older person
  - Services to support family carers
- Length of time for which support is provided, e.g. Czech long-term care units put a limit of months on residence, in Greece the Urban Workers Fund limited public funding for nursing or clinic care to 6 months.

The public sector is increasingly funding and arranging the financial coverage for care but devolving at least some aspects of hands on care to others, be they voluntary, private or family carers, e.g. Hungary has seen a major expansion in NGO provision, the Netherlands leaves it to the older person to arrange what type of care they seek.

2.5.2 Approaches to Carer Support

How can family carers be supported to continue providing care at home for their dependent older people without adverse effects on their own physical and mental health or without long term consequences for their income?

In the NABAREs reports the following areas were examined:

- Financial support including payments / benefits (services in kind and services in cash), social and accident insurance and pension contributions
- Services to the older person
- Services to the family carer

As discussed in section 2.2, the variations in social care provision in the 23 national reports appeared to depend largely on whether the state took primary responsibility for the care of dependent older people, or only by default when there was no or inadequate family to care. In the latter case, seeking help from the state automatically implies a "deficiency" in the socially preferred form of family care, which in itself is perceived as reflecting an older person's "value" to society, earned by having and bringing up children within society's expected norms and values. In general, countries where the state takes primary responsibility for care of dependent older people also have higher levels of service provision (DK, FI, LU, NL, NO, SE, UK), but not exclusively, since several countries in which children have the primary responsibility for care still have quite high levels of service provision (AT, BE, BU, FR, DE, MT, PT).

2.5.3 The Rights of Family Carers and their financial Recognition

A number of countries have introduced public financial payments in the form of benefits or long term care allowances to help with the care of the dependent. These may be paid either to the family carers who provide the care as in AT, BE / Flanders and Brussels, CZ, FR, HU, IE, MT, NO, PL, ES, PT, SI, SE and UK, or they may be paid to the older person to pay the person providing the care service (NL and DE), or in some cases to both. Thus in France the National Allowance for Dependency (APA) is paid to 605,000 means tested older people; however, in some cases family carers may also receive a salary.

In Germany the long-term care allowance is means tested and taxed and older people needing care can choose to take the cash (71 %) and organize care themselves, or take it in benefits in kind and use professional services (12 %), while 15 % combine benefits in kind and in cash.

 In wealthy Luxembourg all those needing help are covered by dependency insurance, the amount varying by assessed levels of need. A dependent older person receiving a nursing allowance (23.85 euros per hour) can use up to 7 hours of care per week to pay a family or informal carer; if 7-14 hrs are needed, the service networks must provide half the hours, if more than 14 hours per week are needed they are entirely provided by help services. Annually the dependent older person receives a double nursing allowance to finance respite care and give the family carer time for recreation.

In several countries the amounts actually paid are so low as to not even cover the direct costs of care, e.g. Malta, Hungary.

There are considerable debates on the benefits of paying family carers directly or the older person, with pros and cons for both arguments; paying the family carer directly may not allow flexibility and change in care arrangements and also runs the risk of devolving all care responsibilities onto a single carer, whereas payments to the older person, although seemingly promoting more choice in care, may not be given to the family member providing the most care.

In many countries there is no public and statutory recognition of family carers (ES, PT, EL, PL, MT, BU) so that there is no **entitlement** to any kind of financial payment, to leave from work or for respite care. In practice, even in these countries some reported that those family carers employed in the public sector did have some rights to paid and unpaid leave, though these rights were virtually never exercised in the private sector (PT, SI). Typical of this situation was Portugal where public employees have the right to 15 days per year under the cover of 'family medical certification' to care for an older person, but in the private sector such leave is only available for the care of those under 10 years of age.

In other countries such as Austria and Germany, where increasing recognition is being given to the reconciliation of work and caring through such policies as care leave, reduced hours and the right to re-employment, there were comments that despite the rhetoric, family friendly policies are rare (1 % of companies in Austria) and mainly for those with scarce skills. In Germany, new rights were introduced for working carers to have leave for short periods of up to one year, with or without wage adjustment, but only a few large Companies allow flexible hours or job sharing (AT, DE). In Sweden, the Care Leave Act (1989) ensures that those under 67 years and still in the labour force have the right to paid leave for 60 days to look after a dying family member.

A number of countries, even those without support services for family carers and very limited public recognition of their role, did permit tax relief and exemptions (FR, IE, EL, IT, NL, ES). In Ireland, tax relief was also available when a private carer was employed.

Another minimal financial form of support, mentioned as available to Maltese and UK family carers, was VAT relief on care aids.

 In Ireland carers are eligible both for respite care benefits and for a Back-to-Education allowance when their caring responsibilities end.

2.5.4 Long-term financial Support

The long term consequences for family carers have been noted in many countries. Some countries have moved towards supporting those providing recognised levels of care in order to both support family carers and ensure that in the longer term they do not land up worse off. In some countries, family carers could be officially recognised and employed as carers with a salary, employment benefits, pension and training (DK, FI, FR, IE limited, NO, UK). While these were the most extensive rights, other countries offered social insurance contributions to provide coverage for old age and accidents; pension credits are a recognised way of supporting family carers in a number countries (CZ, LU, NO, UK) while specific mention is made of coverage for accident and injury (AT, FI).

 In Austria preferential insurance terms and pension contributions are given to non-employed family carers in the form of free non-contributory co-insurance with sickness benefits for those receiving the long term care allowance for the more dependent (levels 4-7) with the state paying the employer's contributions.

2.5.5 Formal Service Provision for older People (health, social services, residential)

Adequate and appropriate health and social services provided to older people, both in institutions and at home, are a major factor in supporting the work of family carers and relieving them of the total burden of care. In those countries with a broad spectrum of **home care services** (SE, DE, UK, NO, DK, FI, FR) that maintain and support older people in their own homes as long as possible, family members may have some choice in deciding whether and how much care they wish to undertake, although home help is often limited and does not exclude the need for help from the family. However the demographic projections suggest that the degree of choice that older people and their family carers will have in the future may be dictated by public expenditure restrictions and private means.

In addition to services provided in the home (home-help, meals-on-wheels, personal care etc.), the provision of appropriate accommodation (permanent and temporary residential care, sheltered housing, home adaptations etc.) and transport services can significantly influence and extend an older person's independence and autonomy, despite increasing levels of disability, and this in turn helps family carers.

 The Polish report describes how in some local areas, such as Poznan, initiatives have been undertaken to improve the quality of care and work conditions of family carers, largely as a result of pressure from well-organised self-help groups and NGOs of older people forcing local authorities to assign appropriate funds.

In Northern Italy, there is a current trend towards an increased involvement of market oriented care services, so that users (i.e. older people and their families) "buy" care services from private suppliers that are paid for with public funds through vouchers and care allowances.

At the other end of the spectrum, Greece has no statutory social care services for older people though some home care programmes have developed over the past decades, initially by NGOs and more recently by local authorities; budget restrictions and inadequate funding means that coverage is limited and the services inevitably give priority to dependent older people without family support and with no financial resources to pay for private help.

2.5.6 Services for older People at Home

It is not always easy to distinguish between services primarily intended for the older person but which substantially reduce the problems and difficulties of the work of the family carers, and those services which are directly focused on and of benefit to the family carer. Thus respite care may directly benefit and even be designed for the family carer, yet essentially be a home based service for the older person. A huge range of services supporting older people exists, including general laundry services, special transport services, hairdresser at home, meals at home, chiropodist / podologist, telerescue / tele-alarm (connection with the central first-aid station or relative), telephone service offered by associations for older people (friend-phone, etc.), counselling and advice services for older people, care aids, home modifications, company for older people, social worker, handyman service, incontinence service. (See Annex 4 for the list of services developed from the national reports.)

Malta mentioned having 30 different services for older people, though with the interesting comment that many family carers using home help services felt it to be an admission of their inability to live up to family expectations, leading to an uneasy partnership between them and the formal service providers

For family carers the availability of good **primary health care in the home** is of great importance, as many older people are not well enough to move easily. Many countries (BE, DK, FR, DE, LU, MT, NL, NO, SE, CH and the UK) described their primary health care services as comprehensive, involving health care professionals in systematic outreach programmes, and included services such as palliative care at home (CH), and rehabilitation at home. The UK interestingly stated that the most popular primary health care services for older people were chiropody and the district nurse. In other countries (AT, BU, CZ, IT), primary health service into the home were considered partial with inadequate regional coverage, while other countries described their primary health care services as inadequate (EL, ES, HU, PL, PT, SL).

The French primary health care system gives a legal right to its citizens to such services as hospital-at-home, a paramedical service and the delivery of drugs.

A strong trend noted in most countries was the growth in **day care centres**, whether attached to hospitals, run by local authorities or by NGOs. These centres are of importance where the family carer works, but also for regular respite care particularly in the cases of older people with dementia. In some countries (NO), coverage was relatively well-developed, apart from some of the rural areas, while in other countries it was noted that coverage was very patchy (FR, IT, DE) with expansion being planned (IE, HU, EL) Only in Poland day care centres were actually decreasing in number. However, one should note the existing variations in the percentages using such centres. Belgium reported 0.3 % of those aged 65-70 years rising to 0.7 % for those 75 years and over. The Czech Republic, which had centres that offered day and weekend care, provided coverage for 0.6 % of those aged 65+. Malta had 5 % of it older citizens attending 14 centres, while in Spain coverage was for just 0.11 % of older people. Usage data was presented quite differently in the Netherlands – who reported 13 % of family carers using such centres, while in the UK 32 % of those receiving care went to such centres (day clubs, day care and day hospitals), a figure that went down to 27 % for those aged 85 and over. In Luxembourg, the 7 centres were designed for psycho-geriatric cases.

Home care services have been well established for many years in many countries and a wide range of services may be provided under this rubric including home help services (shopping, cleaning, cooking etc.) and personal care (bathing, cutting toe nails, toileting etc.) – however it was not always clear from the national reports what exact services were included in each category. The data provided shows the usage by the age of the older person - ranging from 1 % of those aged 65 years and over in Italy, to 15 % of those aged 60 and over in Denmark. Other figures demonstrate, not surprisingly, that the percentages rise with increasing age. Denmark, Belgium and Finland commented that the average length of time for home help was just 2 hours per week, and many countries said that the demand was outstripping the supply both as a result of demographic changes but also, for example, with the introduction of long term care allowances which allowed dependent older people to have more access to such a service (AT). This indicates that many countries are facing the choices of how best to ration care to those who are most dependent. In the UK and Ireland, data indicated that those with family carers received less home care than those without a family carer.

In a number of countries including Finland, Sweden and the UK, it was commented on that home help was now given to less people but more intensively, e.g. in the UK 8.1 hours per week, while in Sweden 28 % received home help in the evenings and at night.

Belgium noted that the main beneficiaries were those who were very dependent and on a low income and no doubt similar criteria are used in other countries, which may well account for the growth reported in a number of countries of private home help services; thus even in Denmark with its extensive services, people were paying for additional help. In some countries the costs of using the service meant that some could not afford it (BU).

Local coordination centres were important as a way of ensuring some cooperation between health and social services. In Finland, personal care and service plans are made by multi-professional health and social service teams for persons in continuous need for care and there is an increased focus on the much older person. In Greece, many of the home care services under development are run in conjunction with the existing Open Care Centres for Older People (KAPIs) and provide both some health and social support. In Sweden, comprehensive local authority services provide transportation services, foot care, meals on wheels, security alarms, housing adaptations, handicap aids, etc.

Home help care programmes in Catalonia, Spain, are available in 90 % of the primary health care centres; more than 75 % of these offer carer training and almost 69 % specific "caring for the carer" programmes.

Given the particularly arduous nature of care for those with Alzheimer's disease or DAT related dependency, the development of special services to support family carers is particularly critical. Norway reported that 80 % of all the local authorities provided sheltered units in nursing homes for persons with dementia in 2003, while Belgium, Luxemburg, Sweden and Finland also had good coverage. However, most countries reported that existing facilities are inadequate in terms of coverage and increasing demand (FR, IT, DE, IE).

One bright light for family care work was that many countries reported on the invaluable work done by different NGOs and especially Alzheimer societies, e.g. in the UK they had 25,000 members and 300 centres running quality day and home care services, while in countries like Slovenia and Greece mention was made of the growing importance of the Alzheimer societies, particularly when other forms of support for older people and family carers were less developed. Only Spain, Poland and Portugal gave no indication of such developments.

Even in Greece, where innovations are hard to implement and public financial support limited and erratic, the GARDA Association in Thessaloniki, supported by Alzheimer Europe, marks dynamic and positive cooperation between health professionals and family carers with effective work in information, advocacy, counselling and service provision in an ever larger number of towns.

Quality Assurance

One way of ensuring that family carers feel that home care services can be safely used and relied on is that adequate quality assurance standards are in place. In many countries, the evaluation and monitoring of the standards of the service provided, whether by health or social care personnel in separate or integrated services, was felt to be inadequate. Many countries also reported that administrative criteria were the main criteria used to judge service adequacy, e.g. legal contract obligations, financial management, staff / client ratios, complaints, while even where local authorities had developed explicit criteria for service providers, these very rarely included the quality of the service from the perspective of the family carer or older person (AT, CZ, IE, DE, EL, PL, ES). What were the constituents of a good quality service assurance? These included national recommendations, the use of independent evaluation and monitoring, clear mission statements, the development of individual client plans drawn up with the older person or family carer, the development of quality awards, and many countries felt they had adequate mechanisms in place (BE, DK, FI, FR, HU, LU, MT, NL, NO, CH, UK, SE). France noted that there were now special computer programmes designed for quality control for both home and residential care services.

In well developed systems it might well be expected that services would devote resources to ensure the level of training and competence of their staff. If European countries are moving to an increase in the number and coverage of both public and private care services in the home, then family carers and older people have to feel confidence in the abilities, commitment and concern of those providing services to the older person. 12 countries considered their staff adequately trained (AT, BE, BU, DK, LU, MT, IT, FI, DE, SE, NL, HU). However, there were differences between the **qualifications of those running services**, who in most countries were trained and with professional certification, e.g. as medical professionals, social workers etc, and those who provide some kinds of hands-on care and support in the home. Austria, Italy and the Czech Republic commented on this issue. The difficulties in recruiting and keeping staff, especially at these levels, have already been discussed in the section on the work of caring (2.4.5). What was often missing was training for home help and geriatric aides. In Spain, the national report sadly pointed to the current inadequacies even amongst those of a professional background, since they often had inadequate profiles for the work, especially in supervision and management; there was also scarce interest by other workers in jobs concerning the hygiene and personal care of the older person and in general a poor connection between the workers and the users of the services. This comment may well have resonance for a number of countries, e.g. FR, SI, CH.

2.5.7 Services for Family Carers

The most common form of service available for family carers was some form of **respite care**, predominantly in residential units with rather fewer offering such care in the older person's or family carer's own home. Respite care services at home probably constitute the most direct and immediate type of relief for family carers, whether this be in the form of 'granny' sitting for a few hours, or for a more extensive period such as a weekend, or to cover a holiday and allow the family carer to relax. Respite care was the only service for family carers reported by **all** the NABARES countries, although there was a very wide variety both in type of provision and coverage. Such services are well developed in a number of countries (BE, NL, NO, SE, UK, DK, FR), whereas in others any form of provision is rare in EL, IT, PL, ES, PT, SI and with more extensive, but still limited coverage in IE, DE, CH, MT. As with many other forms of support for family carers, private arrangements for relief care either at home or in a residential facility, were reported by many countries, either as a substitute for inadequate public services, or in parallel with them.

 In Belgium 10,000 hours of sitting services were provided, a half by volunteers.

 In the Netherlands more than 180,000 hours of voluntary palliative home care were provided at home (more than 5200 volunteers in palliative care). In contrast to formal carers these volunteers do have a lot of time for the family carers.

Given the bureaucratic nature of many of the public systems by which family carers can access services or claim financial support either for themselves or for the older person directly, a major problem for many is how to fill in the right forms. Thus counselling and advice services that helped with such things as filling out forms were surprisingly prevalent amongst many of the 23 countries and 8 reported this as available throughout their country.

 In Austria a provider of in-home hospice services (Caritas) offers a support programme for carers after the death of the older person.

Practical training in caring was available widely, where family carers learned to protect their own physical and mental health, relaxation etc. (IE, SE, MT,

NL, FI, FR, AT, BE, and the UK). A number of these were run by carer's groups or NGOs. Many of these services overlapped with self help groups, designed to allow family carers to learn from one another how to deal with problems and the emotional and practical aspects of caring.

Needs assessment by a service provider, providing a formal and standardised assessment of the caring situation, was a well developed service with total coverage in DE, DK, FI, HU, BE, NL, SE, CH, UK, LU, partial availability in BU, CZ, DE, ES, IE, MT, NO, PL. but not available in AT, CH, EL, FR, IT, PT, SI, although the extent to which family carers were involved in these assessments was not always clear.

However, **integrated planning** of care for older people and their families, which should be a logical next step from needs assessment, was available in fewer countries, with total availability reported only in SE, UK, FI, HU and LU.

Whilst a number of countries reported **special services for family carers of different ethnic groups,** this was a statutory service only in the UK and even here was still not fully developed.

Other support services for family carers were reported by NL, HU and LU.

In Hungary, the vital role of NGOs such as the Hungarian-Maltese Charity service and the Hungarian Red Cross in providing numerous services for older people and their families was noted. Free food, clothing, medicine, medical and technical aids were provided where needed, using both state and other sources of funding and a large amount of volunteer work.

In the Netherlands, the important contribution made by the 200 Support Centres for Family Carers (information and advice, practical and emotional support, training, mutual support groups, and voluntary home care and buddy care) was noted, as well as the wide variety of support services provided by LOT, the Dutch organization for informal caregivers.

2.6   Residential and Long-Term Care

In this section, long-term care usually refers to institutional care provided and funded by the health sector, whilst residential care is usually provided by the social services sector with partial or full costs born by the user. However, it was not always clear from the NABARES reports which were being referred to and thus there may be some overlap between the uses of the two terms. From the point of view of the family carer and the older person needing care, however, whether this type of care is provided free or for payment is obviously a major factor in decisions regarding the use of the service and may partly explain differences in patterns of use of institutional care facilities between countries.

While it would appear slightly contrary to discuss residential care and family care simultaneously, the availability and quality of different forms of residential care for dependent older people helps determine the role of family carers and the types of support they can find. There are different developments in the 23 countries that depend in great part on historic levels of provision; those with low levels are often seeing a growth in new residential units to deal with demographic changes, while those who already have high levels are diversifying the forms of residential coverage available. Increasing longevity accompanied by age-related disability (even taking into account some decline in rates of severe disability) means that a higher number of older people will require care for longer periods of time; this, combined with the predicted decline in numbers and availability of younger generation family carers, means that inevitably an increasing proportion of older people will require the intensive care services only available in an institutional setting. This is already becoming apparent with many countries reporting a high proportion of more disabled older people and those without families in residential care.

An increasingly wide range of institutional care arrangements are reported, with a general trend in those countries with more developed services to move away from traditional residential care and rest homes, nursing homes and short and long term hospital care and convalescent homes, towards other forms of living units such as sheltered housing, specialised rehabilitation facilities, hospice and palliative care facilities and special dementia units and special facilities such as respite care (AT, BE / Flemish, NL). This has led to a less rigid classification of types of institutional care, with merging of the boundaries between health and social care and between home and residential care, i.e. towards more integrated care.

There is a wide mix of public, private and non-profit provision, with most public and NGO facilities, except hospital beds, being run by or in co-operation with local authorities. The highest level of residential care was reported in the Netherlands with 5 % of those aged 65 years and over in residential care homes and 2.5 % in nursing homes, and Luxembourg with 6.8 % of those aged 65 years and over. The lowest rate was reported in Greece with an estimated 1.5 %. Overall, as many countries indicated there is an increase in both the age and level of dependency of older people, as well as the proportion of dementia sufferers, in all types of residential care and there are often waiting lists, especially for specialist and modern units, e.g. Belgium has long waiting lists for dementia patients. However, in interesting contrast, Finland reports a decline in need for institutional care due to improved functional capacity of those 65 and over. In Italy, a decline by half in the percentage of over 85 year

olds in residential care has been attributed primarily to the employment of foreign home care workers.[15]

There are significant cultural differences in the preferences of older people
themselves for this type of care, though the time at which they were asked
about their preferences as well as the wider socio-economic conditions in
which they find themselves, also influences their responses. The critical issue
is what they prefer when they can no longer care for themselves: nine out of
ten Norwegian older people preferred a residential setting, while the Swiss
also preferred professional care. Similar tendencies can be found in the Czech
Republic, Poland, Slovenia and Hungary, where older people in need for care
are put on waiting lists for admission and expanding long-term care and residential facilities.[16]

While many countries reported a policy trend away from institutional care towards home care, some countries with high levels of mainly publicly funded
residential care provision (AT, DK, SE) have not changed bed provision but
have expanded other forms of residential care, e.g. sheltered housing in Norway, with a consequent decline in bed shortages in nursing homes. In Denmark, the decline in nursing home beds has been matched by an increase in
independent specialised housing units for older people with accompanying
home care services, whereas Sweden covers all types of residential care under the umbrella heading "special housing", entry being by criteria of need
only, with a very high public service coverage and a wide variety of accommodation, balanced by improved and integrated home services provision. Finland
has service housing with 24 hr assistance costing two thirds less than traditional residential care and three quarters less than hospital care. In Spain,
where residential care covers 3.4 % of over 65 year olds, the national report
suggests an increase in public sector residential care. Malta and Germany
noted increases in the demand for all types of residential accommodation, and
in Germany residents consist increasingly of the older age groups and dementia sufferers. Even in Greece, despite the use of migrant workers and the start
of some home care services, there has been a small increase in use of residential care services (mostly private) from < 1 % to 1-2 % of > 65 year olds. A
similar situation occurs, to a varying extent, in Italy, although there is a higher
proportion of older people in residential care in the north than the south. Luxembourg, with a currently high level of residential care provision, is expanding
provision further and the report notes that the cost for such care per hour
(35.82 euro) is actually cheaper than home care (48 euro).

In France, as in other countries, there are significant problems with many existing residential homes, some of which are based on the old 'poor-houses',

---

[15] See http://www.esf.org/articles/201/Famsuparticle.pdf
[16] It is not entirely clear if this is because of established traditions or because of the difficult economic
circumstances of both families and older people.

though the development of new forms of small support residential and modern units is making some forms of residential care far more attractive.

 In France and the Walloon part of Belgium the Cantous are special small units for older people with dementia where they share daily life and cooking activities under supervision. The family is involved in decision making and social life.

The **costs of residential care** clearly play an important role for family carers and older people since in many countries the older person or their family contributes or completely pays for this service. In the Czech Republic, long-term care was free and a dependent person received their entire pension plus any dependency allowance. In Denmark, rent was payable for the accommodation only, while care services were free. Long term care allowances awarded in line with assessed levels of disability and need were mainly used in Austria and Germany to cover the costs of residential care. A large number of countries had some forms of mixed payment – Switzerland, Hungary, Malta, Poland, Norway, Finland, and the Netherlands used various forms of means tested and co-payment according to the older person's pension, though ensuring that the older person was left with some disposable income. In France, Ireland and the UK, older people in residential care were often publicly funded, though assets had to be used to pay part or all of the costs. Thus the amount of public subsidy for residential care varied considerably amongst countries. In most cases the poorest and most dependent may get subsidised, as in Spain, though 58.8 % are financed entirely by the user. In Slovenia, 66 % is funded by older people and family carers. In both Greece and Portugal the percentage paid for by the older person is even higher and NGO and religious charities mainly accommodate the isolated and those on a very low income. In Italy, only 5 % of residential accommodation is free.

In Luxembourg residents pay the full cost of care, while in Sweden they pay the costs of rent, meals and care with a cap on the costs for care; in both cases high incomes and pensions and state subsidies for those in need mean that the costs are not a barrier to usage.

The funding of long term care in some countries may actually favour institutional care, e.g. in Italy and the UK, long-term health care facilities may be free or partially covered as opposed to payment for social care facilities, which is means tested or completely privately paid by older people or family carers; in Belgium / Flanders family care at home may be more expensive than residential care; for family carers in the Czech Republic, residential care may allow them to benefit from the older person's pension, even if this involves moving the older person every 3 months to different facilities to avoid paying costs.

Overall many countries noted the decreasing length of public hospital stay for older people with increasingly earlier discharge after acute admissions, e.g.

Hungary. This puts increasing strain on both family carers and on home care services which have to provide higher levels of home care, e.g. UK.

While national and local governments may wish to limit public expenditure and older people and family carers prefer home or sheltered housing with home help services, as indicated care for dependent older people may cost a lot if they are kept in their original homes. There is no consensus of the optimum method of funding residential services and in many countries the choices available in different types of care facilities are very limited.

2.6.1 Sheltered Housing Units

Sheltered housing units are currently not available in a number of countries (BU, EL, HU, PL). Portugal noted the conversion of many of the older residential homes into sheltered units, while Slovenia noted that though they have started there, there was reluctance amongst older people to sell the property and move into these relatively expensive dwellings. Both sheltered and other forms of residential accommodation offering support services are growing in most countries though they tend to be limited to those who are mentally disabled in Luxemburg, while in Norway older people with dementia may be accommodated in sheltered units in nursing homes. In the UK, figures showed 3.5 % of those aged 65+ in such housing, a figure that rises to 19 % for those aged 85 years and over. Again this availability of choice for the older person and family carer is important since the older person retains a home and independence though with appropriate 24 hour available support.

2.6.2 Hospices and palliative Care

Hospices and palliative care may be important for family carers, offering a specialist service to those needing terminal care and allowing both the older person and the family carers to get good psychological and physical care. They are not available in a number of countries including BU, EL and ES. In many countries such forms of service developed under the auspices of NGOs; thus the Czech Republic has 6 new units with 170 beds. In total, 11 countries mentioned the existence of hospices and palliative care, within residential units and in the community. Focussing on hospices and palliative care, the importance of enabling family carers to continue care also in the terminal phase and to avoid institutionalisation must not be disregarded. Specifically, aspects like dignity and cost need to be reflected.

2.6.3 Residential Respite Care

As suggested in the earlier section (2.5.7), many countries de facto offer respite care, whether in specially designed units or as ad hoc arrangements.

In Bulgaria the widespread summer camps are sometimes used for the care of the dependent older person while the family carers take a holiday break.

2.6.4 Training and Quality Control and Family Carer Involvement

As discussed under home care services, the issue of training of care staff and quality control of residential care services is critical, particularly in those countries with low usage. As with home care services, some countries employed a majority of skilled trained staff with the tendency for the less skilled categories of professional carer to be the ones with the least training or continuous education. The Czech report indicates the importance of this issue since the dependency levels in their institutions is worsening.

Again there is a tendency in many countries for administrative criteria to be used to asses quality standards, e.g. they focus on health and safety, staff-resident ratios, space and facilities. However ISO standards have begun to be introduced and were mainly regulated by local authorities (UK has twice yearly inspections, one unannounced and reports are published – the Care Standards Act now sets national standards). FI implements repeat questionnaires for client feedback on quality i.e. availability, adequacy and functionality of services.

The involvement of family carers in residential care services appears to be increasing in Malta and the Netherlands and in Norway cooperation between staff and family caregivers is encouraged. This is partly due to changes from traditional forms of residential care to a wider variety of services, many of which involve family carers (respite care, shared care, etc.) and partly due to changing attitudes to and perceptions of care for older people. In Poland, Italy and Greece, family carers are often encouraged or even obliged to supplement and supervise residential care services that are inadequate due to lack of or indifferent, non-trained staff. Increasing budget cuts for residential care means that family carers and volunteers are increasingly needed to provide all forms of care (NL).

Additionally, family carers are increasingly concerned with the quality of care and feel themselves "partners in care" with formal service providers.

2.7   Current Policy Trends and Debates

Given the very different economic and welfare situations in each of the 23 countries, the discussions and the sophistication of social policy debates being held at local or national level vary enormously. This was particularly the case with respect to family care. Each national expert was asked to report on the state of debate on family care in their country and, though their comments may not be comprehensive they indicate what trends are occurring in each country.

As should be clear, in a number of countries a discussion or policy debate on the issue of family care does still not take place. While in most of these countries (PL, EL, SI, MT, BU) this is the outcome of there being an assumption of the 'normalcy' of family care and / or laissez faire public welfare policy towards citizens, in the case of Denmark the lack of discussion is for the opposite reason, namely the policy of total state care for all dependent older persons. Other countries reported some growing consciousness of the likely increase in demand for support from the public sector as a result of the increasing numbers of older people and the difficulties faced by family carers (BE, CZ, IT, FR, HU, CH). Unless family carers and older people are within a very well developed welfare state, it appears that those with increased incomes turn to private solutions. Many public authorities essentially limit themselves to reactions to crisis rather than being proactive in the support of family carers. However, whether the state has primary responsibility for the care of older people or whether families or the individuals themselves bear the weight of care, there is some convergence in awareness of the need for shared care (public and family), whatever the starting point.

Not surprising given the demographic developments, public debate in many countries is concerned with how the public sector would be able to cover the costs of long term care of older people (FR, IE, BE, EL, NL, NO, SE, AT, LU, DK). The central debate revolves around who should pay - whether this should be funded through new taxation and new forms of social insurance and whether these should be public or private and born primarily by the older person and / or his / her family. The Austrian, German and Dutch evaluation underway of the effects and costs of the long term care insurance scheme will help countries like Spain and France who are considering setting up LTCI.

Providing adequate financial incentives to increase the numbers of individuals willing to provide family care is a debate in Switzerland (whether payments are made directly to the family carer or indirectly through the older person) and the current very low levels of reimbursement in a number of countries such as Austria is clearly no incentive. However, as referred to in the next section, any system of payment for family care will require adequate, continuous and objective needs assessment of the older person if family carers are to be paid from the public purse.

As suggested in an earlier section, enforcing the provision of hands on care by the children of older people appears to be, in practice, unworkable; even making children take financial responsibility for dependent parents is difficult to implement, as illustrated by the current policy debate in Ireland, despite the fact that the country still has larger families to draw on for the financial support of their older members, as well as growing wealth. Italy was involved in a policy debate about whether payments to family carers were preferable to payments to the older person; both these systems were found amongst the 23 countries and it was evident that each had some drawbacks.

Much larger social issues are the central point of policy debates in many coun-tries. Thus the Lisbon agreement to increase labour force participation rates, especially those of women, throughout the member states of the EU has clear repercussions for the practical day to day support of older dependent people and indeed all types of home care. Will women in the future be willing to un-dertake both paid and unpaid care to the same degree, particularly in those countries that currently mainly rely on family care? In countries where family care issues are high on the agenda, defending carers' rights to equality is a major policy debate; this has been particularly successful in Ireland where dis-crimination legislation also covers family carers as workers.

In Portugal the rapid social changes that are occurring are leading to a debate on individualism, life style changes and what they mean in terms of family care. The wealth of Norway has allowed them to provide both good services for older people without devaluing the place of family carers, by clarifying the roles of service providers and family carers in the provision of home care for the very dependent. As the Austrian report makes clear, those with better edu-cation and with better jobs are less willing to provide hands-on-care, a trend that will most likely be repeated throughout Europe. However, the OASIS study suggests that, given adequate services, family carers may be better able to provide more emotional, recreational and psychological support, thus, main-taining and improving the personal relationship between family carer and older person.

Malta and the Czech Republic were involved in policy debates concerning how they could change social attitudes towards ageing and promote greater inde-pendence amongst older people, which would also aid family carers. Nonethe-less, however much there is a chronological postponement of ageing, ulti-mately the fear of death and dependency at the end of life give a negative aura and set of attitudes. As the UK mentioned there is still the problem of the frail, ill and dependent older people and how to make positive social values out of this stage of the life course. The specialist role of residential facilities and hos-pices who may best be able to promote a positive image and experience about the end of life, "a good death" for older people and their family carers, was not mentioned directly in the reports, though the growth of hospices and their wide public support suggests that they may have started to play such a role.

The issue of family care has different advocates in some of the 23 countries. The strength of the family care associations and related NGOs in Ireland and the UK as well as in Finland and in the Netherlands is reflected in the fact that they are major stakeholders in the debates about the support of family carers, while in Italy it is the pensioners organizations who have taken on this policy issue with the regional and central governments.

A number of countries pointed to the fact that the main policy debates con-cerned the provision of more services even though, as in Luxembourg they were already relatively well off. There the main focus of the debate was on the need for more rehabilitation services, palliative and hospice care and more trained workers. In others (CZ, ES, HU), the pressing need for more home care services for older people was the main focus, including more respite care services at home (NL). With regard to the latter, countries with the same policy concern could benefit from an evaluation of systems implementing respite care at home using voluntary or semi-paid substitute carers. Finland, with already good services in place, was involved in policy debates about introducing more flexibility in care to cover different levels of disability. A number of countries reported policy debates on how best to improve the status of family care work and ensure cooperation between family carers and the professionals in the provision of health and social services. This included the debate on whether and how to make family carers municipal workers (BE, FI, NL, AT, IE) as part of the team of care workers, thus blurring the traditional divisions between formal and informal care provision and the private and public spheres of life. Inevitably this had repercussions in the conclusion that more training would be needed for family carers (NL, DE).

Assuring good quality control for services for older people and family carers was a major issue in several countries (IT, EL, NO, DK). The development and implementation of ISO standards for both residential and particularly home care services where supervision is more difficult, would appear to be an important area for cross country co-operation within the EU, through both research and the open method of co-ordination.

The issue of need for legal guardianship for frail older people was reported by Italy and Luxembourg and, taking the issue further, Finland and the UK noted the need for judicial and advocacy support for both family carers and cared for older people. In response to this problem, Poland has developed good legal protection for older people against financial abuse, but it should also be noted that both family carers and older people would benefit from clear legislation in the form of contracts ensuring fair exchanges and payments in return for care, with due protection for the older person's rights.

The detection, prevention and management of elder abuse was a policy debate in Austria and Belgium, and there are strong indications in the NABARES reports that this is of concern widely within Europe. It is also a major concern amongst policy makers in the USA.

3 Conclusions and Policy Implications

Despite the fact that many countries in Europe still do not acknowledge the role of family carers in the social and health support of older people, it should be evident from this report that politicians and policy makers at local, national and EU levels ignore the changing demographic structure of Europe at their peril!

The frequently mentioned 'burden' and spiralling costs for the care of dependent older people can only be confronted by utilising all available resources in a partnership approach to care. The four sectors of the welfare diamond (public, voluntary, family and private) concerned with the provision of care for older dependent people need to find a new balance in ways of working together, based on clearly agreed areas of responsibility. The policy in the EU to encourage the labour market participation of women, including older women, will further reduce the already diminishing pool of family carers able to devote adequate time to hands on care and many ad hoc forms of care currently utilised to fill this gap may not be the best solutions. The public sector, already responsible in large part for the health care of its population, needs to take a proactive role in the allocation of responsibility and the development of support for family carers.

Policy implications and recommendations are derived from the NABARES reports and what the national experts initially considered to be critical in their country for the support of family carers. However, the countries mentioned in the footnotes for each issue are in no way exhaustive and many authors subsequently commented that only their need to be selective had limited the inclusion of many of the other topics listed below. These and other issues emerge as areas where action might effectively be taken at the EU or at national and local levels for the support of family carers. This section covers issues concerned with types of support for family carers, service organization and provision and, critically, the way in which family care can be an integral and acknowledged element in the care for dependent older people within the wider context of labour market policies.

The authors hope that the ideas discussed in this report, and the policy implications summarised below, will stimulate thinking on how best each country can innovate and find solutions for the support of family carers.

3.1 More Services for Family Carers and older People

■ Encourage innovation in providing new services for family carers and older people[17]

---

[17] BE, UK, EL, AT

- More short term and flexible respite care[18]

- More medium and longer term respite care centres[19]

- More day care[20]

Respite care is a key service in those countries where family carers undertake a lot of practical care. Consideration should be given to ways of covering long and irregular working hours for working carers including 24 hour and week-end care.

> The trend in more advanced countries to have a variety of forms of flexible and attractive residential care to suit the various needs of both dependent older people and their family carers is one that needs to be systematically developed in more countries.

- More palliative care[21]

- Palliative care[22]

The emergence of palliative care as a specialty both as a home and residential service, can alleviate the problems and concerns of both older people and their family carers and contribute to optimum care at the end of life. The role of humanitarian and religious organisations in this area of care should be expanded.

> The promotion of local or regional Centres of Excellence which include training for family carers and professionals in palliative and end of life care.
>
> Collaborative work with humanitarian and religious organizations at EU level.

- More formal, publicly supported home care services, e.g. home nursing, home help[23]

- More provision of specialised services at home, e.g. dental care, diagnostic services, rehabilitation, chiropody[24]

- Structures (financial, administrative) to support those with long term health care needs (ambulatory, residential and psychiatric)[25]

The wide disparities in the provision and coverage of home care services for older people in the 23 countries of the NABARES reports, underlines the inequalities currently experienced by family carers.

---

[18] AT, DE, IT, IE, EL, NL, SI
[19] AT, DE, EL
[20] FR, PL
[21] AT, DE
[22] HU, PT
[23] HU, PT, NO, FI, CZ, EL, PL, SI
[24] PT, EL, SI, NO, FI, CZ
[25] PT, CZ, EL

Within the EU the open method of co-ordination could stimulate member states to consider how to make the coverage of home care services more extensive as well as methods of funding such services.

The extension of specialist services into the home requires the development of new technologies and lightweight equipment; the recognition of the market demand for such services may stimulate the private sector. The experiences of countries such as Finland with well developed public home health care services would be valuable.

Professional concern with the issue of long term health care at home is currently at the centre of much discussion both at national and international levels (Groves and Wagner 2005, WHO 2005, WHO 2003)

The cost benefits of all forms of prevention and rehabilitation would be a good area for EU research and development.

- Meeting needs of those with dementia including more special residential care units and disseminating knowledge about dementia[26]

The important work of the Alzheimer Associations and groups throughout Europe was noted in most reports in the promotion of carers' interests. This is an example of positive cooperation and an excellent multiplier effect when professionals and family carers work together.

- The effective development of services in rural areas[27]

Most countries in Europe have rural areas with high proportions of older people and difficulties in extending services into these areas at a reasonable cost. Hungary has managed under difficult economic circumstances to develop networks of support using neighbours, friends and volunteers.

Cooperative research on the most effective and economic forms of support for OP in rural areas

- More home renovations and adjustments[28]

Using local resources and local staff to implement home modifications that aid family carers and dependent older people is a valuable and economically feasible service that could be provided by all local authorities.

3.2 Financial Support

- Financial support for family carers regardless of other financial support, e.g. widow's pension[29]

---

[26] AT, DE, BE, EL, IE, FR
[27] NO
[28] FI
[29] FI, CZ, EL, SI

The short and long term benefits and their implications for the public purse of providing different forms of financial support for carers was not clear from the NABARES reports.

> The short and long term benefits of varying forms of financial support to family carers is an important issue where exchanges of experience at EU level may be contribute to evidence based policy making.
>
> Ensuring that family carers are adequately covered by social insurance (accidents, health, pensions etc) during the time spent caring should be a minimum EU standard contributing to the reduction of long term poverty amongst those who undertake family care.
>
> Linking obligatory training to payments for care, as in Finland, helps to ensure both quality in care provision and adequate incomes for family carers.

- Encourage business sponsorship and other donors to fund support services[30]

The issue of how to fund services is critical for the majority of countries and mixed solutions need to be experimented with.

> The exchange of information amongst EU countries on innovative and mixed forms of funding of services should be encouraged.

- Tax allowances and benefits for family carers [31]

These exist in many countries, though often in lieu of any other form of support.

> National governments can use tax declarations as a way of estimating the numbers of householders claiming to look after dependent older relatives.

- Develop Long Term Care Insurance[32]

The central issue is that of funding and the willingness of governments and citizens to bear the generally increased costs through indirect or direct taxation. The Austrian, Dutch, German and also the Japanese experience will be valuable.

3.3 Working Carers

- Promoting flexible workplace practices for family carers[33]

> Development of part-time work in line with needs of both the employer and employee.

---

[30] BU
[31] FI
[32] FR
[33] AT, DE, IT, FI, UK, SI

The development of comprehensive labour market policies to include "caring as a lifetime resource" within the context of reconciling work and family life, e.g. part time work for both men and women with full pension and insurance credits for specified periods of time devoted to the care of children, dependent adults and older dependent people.

3.4 NGOs, Advocacy, Information, legal Advice, Counselling

■ More information for family carers and older people[34]

This issue also emerged as important for family carers in the national surveys undertaken in the 6 core countries. All four sectors concerned with family care have an important, if different, role to play in the provision of information. Linking with successful disease-specific groups (Alzheimer, Parkinson's, diabetes, etc.), as well as NGOs and advocacy groups to develop common interests and issues promotes effective collaboration and outcomes.

The proposed EUROCARERS NGO may consider making web and other links to existing NGOs and disease specific groups to promote general knowledge and common policy issues, e.g. service standards, effective support for family carers.

The vulnerability of many older dependent people and also family carers to exploitation and abuse needs to be addressed through adequate public legislation that several countries have already put in place.

Examination of legal issues relating to family care at EU level, e.g. guardianship, financial abuse.

■ Not to shift financial costs of care to family carers [35]

The promotion of the EU Carers' Charter of Rights aims to protect family carers.

■ Support formation of carers' groups [36]

The founding of a EUROCARERS group may help to give the issue a European wide profile, but changing mind sets is not easy.

■ Promotion of family care as work [37]

One debate is whether policy development for family carers of older people should be included with that of family carers of dependent people of all ages. Unified policies have the advantage of avoiding age discrimination in support for family carers of older people, though the younger disabled may feel that

---

[34] BE, BU, FI, EL, PL
[35] FR
[36] MT, EL, SI
[37] NL

public resources for their family carers may be 'diluted' by the increasing needs of older dependent people.

> The current discussion at EU level for the adoption of compulsory social insurance for family carers providing assessed levels of care above, e.g. 18 hours per week, is a positive development.

- Targeted public relations to promote public recognition of family carers[38] and support civil society (NGO) initiatives [39]

National, local and EU support for family carers advocacy groups is a way of promoting partnership between the sectors involved in family care.

> The continuing financial and political support of the EU for organizations such as those in the Social Platform (including AGE), as well as others of relevance, is critical for their survival.

3.5 Formal Labour Force

- Incentives to increase recruitment into nursing and care work with older people by raising the status and improving the conditions of employment [40]
- Targeting men

The evidence from a number of countries suggests that poor recruitment and retention in care work can be successfully overcome, although this may be partly dependent on the national economic situation and the labour market. Improving the training and status of the work as well as conditions of employment are key elements to success. The recruitment of men as care workers may aid in the improvement of the status and wages of care work.

> Scholarships for those in residential and other caring work.
>
> Well-funded chairs in gerontological nursing and geriatric medicine
>
> The development of EU recognised training standards and programmes for care workers.
>
> In conjunction with national training schemes advertising campaigns by national governments to promote a better image of care work. Such a campaign may also choose to target men as care workers.

- Optimize the recruitment of migrant care workers at all levels and regulate the private care services [41]

---

[38] DE, IT
[39] HU, PT, IE
[40] BE, DE, BU
[41] DE, IT, EL

The significant role of migrant care workers suggests the need for more measures not only to regulate and legalise their status but also to ensure their training. The current unregulated use of migrants as private care workers in many countries is a temporary solution for the privileged middle classes as a response to a lack of public policy and services.

Encouragement of more EU training programmes to support migrant care service enterprises and migrant care workers training.

- Innovative practices and new technologies including the legal basis to help with assistive technologies and IT [42]

The EU is already experimenting with IT and assistive technologies for older people and family carers.

Continued and increasing EU investment in research and dissemination of technologies that can aid care work and the organization of services.

3.6 Needs Assessment

- Systematic carer assessments[43]
- Care work involves a wide range of tasks in addition to support for household tasks and personal care, e.g. dealing with officials, financial support, gardening, accompanying.[44]

It is important to include all these areas in the needs assessment although this assumes the development of at least some appropriate support services for family carers or older people. A clear agreement on responsibilities between professionals and family carers for the various caring tasks is needed at the service level (see also section 2.5.7 on integrated care).

National and EU standardised comprehensive needs assessment procedures should be developed for older people, which include assessment of the role and needs of the family carer[45]. We need feedback on the effectiveness of existing systems.

3.7 Promotion of Health and Well-being for Family Carers

- Gender-sensitive health promotion and prevention for family carers[46]

---

[42] IE
[43] UK
[44] HU, DE
[45] The COPE Index, CAMI, CASI and CADI are all validated carer assessment instruments. http://www.shef.ac.uk/sisa/index.html
[46] DE, IE, UK

The promotion of well being amongst family carers also contributes to an improved well being of the older people they care for. Although the national governments and the EU have worked on health promotion with respect to older people, less has been done for family carers.

Public authorities and policy makers should work closely with the media (e.g. public television and radio stations) to develop programmes aimed at family carers at home (skills training, counselling advice, chat shows, information)

■ Provide more counselling for family carers[47]

Feedback is needed on the effectiveness and cost benefit of counselling in preventing carer depression and break down and in the promotion of carer's well being.

■ Programmes to support autonomy of OP[48]

An important issue in many countries where older people traditionally expect to receive family care and may not appreciate their own role in maintaining their physical and mental independence and well being.

Local authorities could contribute through a variety of programmes promoting active social participation of older people and their family carers.

3.8 Evaluation and Monitoring

■ Involve family carers and older people in monitoring services improving evaluation[49]

Develop EU project on methods of effective, efficient and easily implemented evaluation for service providers and family carers.

ISO standards for all types of care services at EU level need to be implemented and encouraged in all European countries as a way of promoting quality evaluation. This is an important area for cross country cooperation in the development of standards

■ Supporting the national registration of family carers[50]

The difficulties of defining family carers are general and though a national register would help there has to be a real incentive to register.

---

[47] UK
[48] PT
[49] UK, DK, SE
[50] MT

3.9   Integrated Care and Training

3.9.1 Professionals

■ Better co-ordination between different providers (usually health and social services), including any necessary legal provisions for cooperation between them[51]

Incentives for the provision of integrated care are being widely discussed by policy makers and professionals, e.g. the CARMEN Network http://www.ehma.org/projects/carmen.asp

■ Better links between home and institutional care – integrated care (cooperation between multi-professional teams and family carers as team members).[52]

Integrated training needs to include decision makers and managers, as well as care workers and trainees.

■ More training in the care of older people as well as training in team work for general medical practitioners[53]

Integrated care involves training in working as a member of a team that includes family carers where relevant, and promotes links between sectors and improving geriatric knowledge.

Abolishing barriers to joint working between health and social services for older people is critical to the promotion of flexible and person centred care.

Higher education and continuous professional training institutes need to incorporate training in integrated care for all professional team members (health and social service personnel and other support staff).

3.9.2 Family Carers

■ More training for family carers and care support services[54]

■ More training for family carers in multidisciplinary teams[55]

The "caring professions", e.g. doctors and nurses, learn how to provide good professional care services without too much emotional involvement. Family carers, especially those providing a lot of hands on care, can be taught to "professionalize" some caring tasks allowing them to be more effective and efficient and to protect their own health. As well as organised training pro-

---

[51] AT, BE, BU, HU, IE, PT, NO, PL, ES, FI, CZ, SI and DE (with respect to discharge.)
[52] AT, BE, BU, DE, UK, CZ, EL, NL, ES, PL, SI
[53] BE, BU, DE
[54] AT, DE, BU, PT, FI, UK, CZ, EL, FR, SI
[55] FI, PL

grammes, outreach 'on-the–job' training for family carers in the home by professionals is a practical and necessary alternative.

Health authorities should set up mechanisms, e.g. case conferences, outreach
programmes, for the active and informed inclusion of family carers in integrated teams.

Training programmes for family carers need to be more widely developed and
routinely include home based training by professionals (learning by doing).

3.9.3 Volunteers

■ More training for volunteers[56]

■ Further development of training concepts for volunteers working with family
carers and older people[57]

*The importance of volunteer work with family carers of older people is highly
variable between the 23 countries. They may be particularly important in sub-
stituting for family carers in the lighter forms of home care services, e.g. shopping, cooking, errands, as well as granny sitting and short term respite. Given
the noted tendency for home care services to concentrate more on the most
dependent section of the elderly population this form of volunteer support may
have increasing value for family carers in the future. Consideration needs to be
given to methods of increasing and 'professionalizing' some volunteer work so
that it becomes a reliable service as well as informal arrangements. The partial
payment of trained volunteer groups may provide particular social value to
their work and help in the development of more extensive volunteer services in
some countries. The role of organised volunteer work in supporting family carers has been under-researched particularly regarding the relative importance
of different forms of volunteer service.*

Local authorities responsible for the development and provision of services for
older people should consider partial funding for organised, trained volunteer
groups.

EU research is needed on evaluating the experiences of countries with voluntary or semi-paid volunteer services, and trained vs. non trained volunteers,
e.g. in the provision of respite care at home.

---

[56] DE
[57] DE

4 References

All the national reports (NABARES) contain their own bibliographies: http://www.uke.uni-hamburg.de/extern/eurofamcare/presentations.html

National Background Reports sorted by Country:

Josef Hörl (2004) National Background Report for Austria

Anja Declerq, Chantal Van Audenhove (2004) National Background Report for Belgium

Lilia Dimova, Martin Dimov (2004) National Background Report for Bulgaria

Iva Holmerová (2004) National Background Report for Czech Republic

George W. Leeson (2004) National Background Report for Denmark

Terttu Parkatti, Päivi Eskola (2004) National Background Report for Finland

Hannelore Jani (2004) National Background Report for France

Martha Meyer (2004) National Background Report for Germany

Liz Mestheneos, Judy Triantafillou, Sofia Kontouka (2004) National Background Report for Greece

Zsuzsa Széman (2004) National Background Report for Hungary

Mary McMahon, Brigid Barron (2004) National Background Report for Ireland

Francesca Polverini, Andrea Principi, Cristian Balducci, Maria Gabriella Melchiorre, Sabrina Quattrini, Marie Victoria Gianelli, Giovanni Lamura (2004) National Background Report for Italy

Dieter Ferring, Germain Weber (2005) National Background Report for Luxembourg

Joseph Troisi (2004) National Background Report for Malta

Reidun Ingebretsen, John Eriksen (2004) National Background Report for Norway

Piotr Bledowski, Wojciech Pedich (2004) National Background Report for Poland

Liliana Sousa, Daniela Figueiredo (2004) National Background Report for Portugal

Simona Hvalic Touzery (2004) National Background Report for Slovenia

Arantza Larizgoita (2004) National Background Report for Spain

Lennarth Johansson (2004) National Background Report for Sweden

Astrid Stückelberger, Philippe Wanner (2005) National Background Report for Switzerland

Geraldine Visser-Jansen, Kees Knipscheer (2004) National Background Report for The Netherlands

Mike Nolan (2004) National Background Report for the United Kingdom

Other References

Albert J and Kohler U (2004) Health care in an Enlarged Europe. European Foundation for the Improvement of Living and working Conditions, Dublin.

Groves T, Wagner E (2005) Editorial: "High quality care for people with chronic diseases" BMJ 2005; 330:609-610

Giddens A (1991) Modernity and Self-Identity: Self and Society in the Late Modern Age, Cambridge, Polity Press

Johansson SL (2004) NABARE Sweden

Magnusson L (2005) "Designing a responsive service for family carers of frail, older people using information and communication technology." Dissertation for Goteborgs universitet, Goteborg,

Pflüger K (2004) "Study into the impact of EU policies on Family Carers". AGE older People's Platform, Brussels.

Pijl M (1994) "When private care goes public: an analysis of concepts and principles concerning payments for care". In Payments for Care: A Comparative Overview. European Centre Vienna, Avebury.

Robine J Romieu I (1998) "Health expectancies in the European Union: progress achieved". REVES Paper 319. INSERM, Montpelier, France.

Theobald H (2003) Social Exclusion and the Care of the Elderly. CARMA (Care for the Aged at Risk of Marginalisation), EU report. Berlin: WBZ Social Science Research Centre.

WHO (2005) Preparing a Health Care Workforce for the 21st Century: The Challenge of Chronic Conditions, WHO Geneva.

WHO (2003) Key Policy Issues in Long-Term Care http://whqlibdoc.who.int/publications/2003/9241562250.pdf

Related Studies and Programmes

CARMEN - the Care and Management of Services for Older People in Europe Network http://www.ehma.org/projects/carmen.asp

EUROCARERS: European Organisation on Informal Care
http://www.york.ac.uk/inst/spru/eurocarers.htm

European Foundation for the Improvement of Living and Working Conditions
http://www.eurofound.eu.int/

European Observatory on the Social Situation, Demography and the Family
http://europa.eu.int/comm/employment_social/eoss/index_en.html

FELICIE - Future Elderly Living Conditions in Europe http://www.felicie.org

IPROSEC - Improving Policy Responses and Outcomes to Socio-Economic
Challenges: changing family structures, policy and practice
http://www.iprosec.org.uk/xnat.html

OASIS - Old Age and Autonomy: The Role of Service Systems and Intergenerational Family Solidarity http://oasis.haifa.ac.il/

PROCARE – Providing Integrated Health and Social Care for Older Persons:
issues, problems and solutions http://www.euro.centre.org/procare/

SHARE - Survey of Health, Ageing and Retirement in Europe
http://www.share-project.org/

SOCCARE – New Kinds of Families, New Kinds of Social Care

http://www.uta.fi/laitokset/sospol/soccare/   *Kröger 2001 - new*
, 2005 ed – Final report

5 Annexes

5.1 Annex 1

5.1.1 NABARES Country List and Abbreviations

1.	Austria	AT
2.	Belgium	BE
3.	Bulgaria	BU
4.	Czech Republic	CZ
5.	Denmark	DK
6.	Finland	FI
7.	France	FR
8.	Germany	DE
9.	Greece	EL
10.	Hungary	HU
11.	Ireland	IE
12.	Italy	IT
13.	Luxembourg	LU
14.	Malta	MT
15.	The Netherlands	NL
16.	Norway	NO
17.	Poland	PL
18.	Portugal	PT
19.	Slovenia	SI
20.	Spain	ES
21.	Sweden	SE
22	Switzerland	CH
23.	United Kingdom	UK

5.1.2 NABARES Analytic Matrices and Abbreviations in Matrices

<	under
>	over
Aut.Com.	Autonomous Communities in Spain
Cos	Companies
FC	family carer
Fed.	Federal
HH	home help
Hrs	hours
HS	Health Services
LA	Local Authorities includes municipalities
LTC	Long term care
LTCI	Long term care insurance
Ltd	limited
NGO	non governmental organization
NI	National Insurance
OP	older person
OW	older women
p.a.	per annum
p.m.	per month
p.w.	per week
PHC	Primary Health Care
Rehab	rehabilitation
SS	Social Services

5.2   Annex 2 – Future Research Needs

Hardly surprising given that the national experts were researchers, when asked to make recommendations on what research was needed, they had a long list of suggestions. The lack of common definitions and standards for gaining data means that national reports are not always easily useable at EU level. Greece, Poland, Portugal and the Czech Republic stated they would be happy to see any national research undertaken on the subject of family care and support services since so little research had been done. Specific suggestions are listed below.

- Longitudinal studies / cohort investigations at a national level. (AU, FR, DK, IT) including the needs and expectations of future cohorts of older people (BE)

- Families as long standing exchange systems; motivation of spouses and descendants to care, not to care and to stop caring (FR, AT, HU)

- organisation and economy of service provision, in particular the balance between public and private provision; issues related to financing, the balance between services, and future planning of services (BG, FIN, NO)

- Empirical studies of elder abuse (AT, FI, FR, DK,UK)

- Action research e.g. aimed at supporting practice, via stepped-care and shared-care methodologies. (AT, BE, UK)

- Paid private care at home, migrant carers and their role as illegal and legal domestic care workers (IT, DK, DE)

- Gender specific aspects of family care (DE, FI, FR, MT)

- Carers in employment, conflicts between care and work, and a comparison with non working carers (FR, SE, UK, MT)

- Young carers (SE, UK)

- Family care and coping in everyday life, positive aspects of caring, strategies to cope with the burden (IE, FR, UK)

- Normative attitudes in society towards caring responsibilities- changing values in relation to income and education and increased female labour market participation (IE, FR, MT)

- Factors determining differences in the awareness of public services and the impact on use (ES)

- Dependence insurance including the evaluation of dependency, degrees of coverage, types of insurance and financing, price and the criteria of determining the right to coverage (ES)

- Caring for persons with rare diseases (SE)

- Caring and ethnic groups and emigrants (SE, FR, DK)
- Validating evaluation procedures to measure user satisfaction in collaboration between the formal care and service system and family care (SE)
- Innovate Case Management and the role of New Public Management in the organising of care of older people and the perspectives of older people and family caregivers.(DE, NO)
- Dementia and family care (DK)
- The use of technology to support family carers and older people and reduce their isolation (UK, IE)
- Carers support in rural settings (SE, FR, NO)
- Outcome of carers support (SE, FR)
- Comparison of care given by co-resident versus non co-resident family carers. (MT)
- Examination of the responsibilities and needs of the 'sandwich' generation of carers (Carers with multiple care obligations (MT)
- Need for "objective" policy proposals based on cost / benefit to all parties

5.3 Annex 3 – STEP for NABARES

The standardised Evaluation Protocol (STEP) for the Reports had the following sections

■ Introduction – An Overview on Family Care – 2-3 pages

■ Data for each country on:

1. Profile of family carers of older people

2. Care policies for family carers and the older person needing care.

3. Services for family carers

   – Good practices

   – Innovative practices in supporting carers.

4. Supporting family carers through health and social services for older people

   4.1. Health and Social Care Services

       4.1.1. Health services – primary, secondary and tertiary care

       4.1.2. Social services – home care services and residential care

   4.2. Quality of formal care services and its impact on family care-givers

   4.3. Case management and integrated care (integration of health and social care services to organise care around the patient / client).

5. The Cost – Benefits of Caring – how much does care cost and who pays

6. Current trends and future perspectives in family caregiving in each country

7. Appendix to the National Background Report

   7.1 Socio-demographic data on older people – Profile of the older population – past trends and future perspectives

   7.2 Examples of good or innovative practices in support services

8. References to the National Background Report

Finally, and most importantly, we asked the authors to write three overviews to be used for national and EU policy recommendations in the final phase of the project with Key Points aimed at:

■ Representative organisations of family carers and older people

■ Service providers

■ Policy makers

5.4   Annex 4 – List of Social Services for Older People

The following services were identified in the reports:

- Permanent admission into residential care / old people's home
- Temporary admission into residential care / old people's home in order to relieve the family carer
- Protected accommodation / sheltered housing (house-hotel, apartments with common facilities, etc.)
- Laundry service
- Special transport services
- Hairdresser at home
- Meals at home
- Chiropodist / Podologist
- Telerescue / Tele-alarm (connection with the central first-aid station or relative)
- Care aids
- Home modifications
- Company for the older person
- Social worker
- Day care (public or private) in community centre or residential home
- Night care (public or private) at home or in a residential home
- Private cohabitant assistant ("paid carer," mainly migrant care workers, legal or illegal)
- Daily private home care for hygiene and personal care
- Social home care for help and cleaning services / "Home help"
- Social home care for hygiene and personal care
- Telephone service offered by associations for older people (friend-phone, etc.)
- Counselling and advice services for older people
- Social recreational centre
- Other, specify

5.5 Annex 5 – Matrix Services for Family Carers for 23 Countries

Services for family carers	Availability			Statutory	Public, Non statutory	Voluntary		Private
	Not	Partially	Totally			Public funding	No public funding	
Needs assessment (formal – standardised assessment of the caring situation)	AT, CH, EL, FR, IT, PT, SI	BU, CZ, DE, ES, IE, MT, NO, PL	BE, CH, DE, DK, FI, HU, LU, NL, SE, UK	BU, DE, DK, FI, HU, LU, MT, NL, NO, PL, SE, UK	ES, BE, IE, PL	ES, IE	HU	
Counselling and Advice (e.g. in filling in forms for help	EL, PT	BU, CZ, DE, ES, FI, FR, IE, IT, MT, NO, PL, SI	AT, BE, BU, CH, DK, HU, IT, LU, NL, SE, UK	BE, BU, CH, CZ, DE, DK, HU, LU, MT, NO, UK	AT, BE, CH, CZ, ES, FI, FR, IE, IT, LU, MT, PL, SE	AT, CZ, DK, ES, DE, FR, IE, IT, MT, PL, SI, UK,	AT, BU, FR, HU, IE, MT, SI	BU, DE, DK, FI, FR, MT, PL, UK
Self-help support Groups	BU, CH, LU, MT	BE, CZ, DE, DK, EL, ES, FI, FR, HU, IE, IT, NO, PL, PT, SI, UK	AT, NL, SE	UK	DE, ES, FI, IT, NL, PL, SE	BE, CZ, DE, DK, ES, FI, FR, IE, IT, NL, NO, PL, SI, UK	AT, BE, EL, FR, HU, IE, IT, NL, NO, PL, PT, SI	AT, DE, DK, FI, FR, PT
"Granny-sitting"	CH, MT, SI	AT, BE, CZ, DE, DK, FI, FR, IE, LU, NL, NO, PL, PT, SE, UK	BU, EL, IT	BU, DE, UK	BE, FI, NL	BE, CZ, DE, DK, FI, IE, NL, UK	BE, BU, EL, FI, HU, IE, LU, NO, PL, SE	AT, BE, DE, EL, FI, FR, IT, DK, PL, PT, UK
Practical training in caring, protecting their own physical and mental health, relaxation etc.	BU, DK	AT, BE, CH, CZ, EL, ES, FI, FR, HU, IE, IT, MT, NL, NO, PL, PT, SI, UK	AT, DE, LU, SE	DE, LU, UK	DE, ES, FI, IT, NL, PL, SE	AT, BE, CH, EL, ES, FI, FR, IE, IT, MT, NL, PT, SI, UK	AT, CZ, FR, HU, MT, NL, NO, PL, PT	FR, PT

Services for family carers	Availability			Statutory	Public, Non statutory	Voluntary		Private
	Not	Partially	Totally			Public funding	No public funding	
Weekend breaks	AT, BU, CZ, DK, EL, MT, SI	CH, DE, ES, FI, FR, HU, IE, IT, NL, NO, PL, PT, SE, SI, UK	BE, LU	DE, FI, LU, SE, UK	BE, ES, IT, NL, PT	BE, CH, DE, ES, IE, NL, UK	HU, NL	BE, DE, ES, FR, IT, NL, PL, PT, UK
Respite care services		AT, CH, CZ, DE, DK, ES, FI, FR, HU, IE, IT, MT, NL, NO, PL, PT, SI, UK	BE, BU, LU, SE	BU, DE, DK, FI, IE, LU, MT, SE, UK	AT, BE, IT, ES, NL, PT, SI	BE, CH, CZ, FR, IE, NL	AT, FR, HU, IE, MT, NL, PT	BE, CZ, ES, FR, HU, IE, IT, NL, PL, PT, SI
Monetary transfers	BE, CH, MT, PL, PT, SI	AT, DK, ES, FI, FR, IE, NL, NO, PT	BU, DE, IT, LU, SE	BU, CZ, DE, DK, FI, IE, IT, LU, NL	AT, ES	IE	AT	FR
Management of crises	CZ, DK, PT	AT, BU, CH, EL, ES, FR, IE, IT, MT, NO, PL, PT, SE, UK	BE, FI, HU, LU	BE, DE, FI, FR, HU, LU, UK	AT, BU, ES, FR, IE, IT, PL, SE	CH, DE, FR, IE, IT, UK	AT, BU, FR, HU, IT, PL	CH, FR
Integrated planning of care for elderly and families (in hospital or at home)	BE, EL, CH, PT, SI	AT, BU, CZ, DK, IE, IT, MT, NL, NO, PL, UK	FI, HU, LU, SE	DE, DK, FI, HU, LU, MT, NL, SE, UK	AT, BU, FI, IE, IT	IE, PL	AT, BU, HU, PL	
Special services for family carers of different ethnic groups	AT, BE, BU, CH, CZ, DK, EL, IE, IT, MT, PL, PT, SI	DE, FI, FR, LU, NL, NO, SE, UK		UK	DE, FI, NL, SE	DE, FI, NL, UK	NL	

Services for family carers	Availability			Statutory	Public, Non statutory	Voluntary		Private
	Not	Partially	Totally			Public funding	No public funding	
Other								
Support Centres for FCs voluntary home care and buddy care, HU- -Maltese Charity service	BU, CH, PL	NL, IE	HU		NL	HU, IE, LU, NL	HU	

5.6 Annex 6 – Matrix of Family Carers' Legal Position and Recognition by State

Country	Legal Obligation	Legal Enforcement of Duties of FC	Rights of FC - pension, leave	Financial recognition	Role of FC and social attitudes
Austria	Spouses legally responsible for one another. In some provinces and defined limits OP can demand maintenance from descendants. Children have to contribute financially in most provinces under social assistance laws for costs of community services / residential care. Excludes Vienna where filial obligation abolished.	Incoherent regulations in different provinces, degree of enforcement is variable. Supreme Admin Court and other legal bodies have made decisions on when provincial bodies can demand cost contribution from family.	Preferential insurance terms for non-employed providing LTC. Self-insurance under health and pension insurance schemes; free non-contributory co-insurance with sickness benefits to carers in receipt of LTC allowance levels 4-7. 1998 FC acknowledged in LTC Act – get pension contributions, state pays employer contributions. Working carers – claim max 1week p.a. for relative in common household. Possibility of getting reduced working Hrs but only 1% Co.s have family friendly policies – mainly for highly qualified. 2002 compassionate leave for dying – 6 month protection from dismissal- unpaid.	Federal LTC allowance 1993 – single case benefit to compensate for care related additional expenses – 7 different levels - consumer directed. Statutory entitlement. Not means tested.	High social expectation of filial and spouse care. De facto most care from families but women with careers less willing to care. Attempts to change social attitudes of employers by the Family and Work Audit. Little co-ordination and co-operation between family members and service providers.
Belgium (Note differences between Walloon and	Financial responsibilities but not to provide care – may include even grandchildren for costs of residential care.	Public Centre for Social Welfare can reclaim costs of residential care from family	Yes	LTCI exists in Flemish part plus incentives to FC for care of those aged 70+. Pays for non medical costs and some LAs	Increasing public acknowledgment of their role. OP perceive families as less willing to care. However FC still critical.

Country	Legal Obligation	Legal Enforcement of Duties of FC	Rights of FC - pension, leave	Financial recognition	Role of FC and social attitudes
Flemish area)				give extra compensation to FCs. Variations between regions. Walloon area LTCI does not exist.	
Bulgaria	Yes	Social services cannot easily collect costs of care back from relatives if not well off.	No	No	Social expectation, but with mass emigration and inadequate services, there are problems.
Czech Republic	Rights and obligations of FCs not legally defined.	OP Right to health care / no right to social care favours institutionalisation and discriminates against FC – also system of reimbursement of GP care favours hospital vs. home care and GPs "reject" dependent OP and their family carers	Pension credits for relative's care	Paid carer's allowance to care for sick family member if unable to work due to caring duties – (1st 9 days x 1 for diagnosis) – complex system but used in areas of high unemployment	1) Ambivalent attitudes to FC by OP and FCs due to conflicts over responsibilities between state and family (socialist vs. traditional). 2) FCs act as managers of care arrangements
Denmark	No	No	legislatively stipulated rights are the right to compensation for lost earnings in case of caring for a dying relative, and the right to employment as a carer when certain conditions are met	No – welfare state funds all provisions.	No role; no expectation. But increasing role and recognition of Familial networks
Finland	No family obligation. Legal obligation of state via municipality to provide care for dependent OP	No	Yes, clearly defined in Social Welfare Act. Days off, rehab and relaxation. Variety of projects.	Yes, by municipality – also Injury Insurance!! Taxable. Amount varies Attendant Carers Allowance. Min 229,29 €	Yes, formal and legal recognition of carer status as part of social and health services Desire by OP and state to increase this
France	Yes, spouses but under	LA can deduct costs in-	Means tested benefits for	Tax benefits	moral expectation of FC –

Country	Legal Obligation	Legal Enforcement of Duties of FC	Rights of FC - pension, leave	Financial recognition	Role of FC and social attitudes
	civil code children are obliged to maintain their mother, father and other ascendants3	curred in care of OP from inheritance	those 60+ national allowance of dependency (APA) to OP. If FC takes salary then there are pension contributions paid. APA beneficiaries = 605,000		by policymakers, society as well as potential and active family carers share, based on the concept of moral obligation due to one's spouse and one's old parents.
Germany	Yes. Filial obligation, but means tested	Means tested	Yes – pension, (580,000 FCs under LTCI) courses in caregiving. Tax benefits. Rights to leave for short periods or for up to one year and can be granted with or without wage adjustment. New – only few large Cos allow flexible hours or job sharing	LTC Allowance. Taxable. Amount varies. Attendance Allowance of min 230 €. 71% of those needing care draw benefits in cash & organize care themselves; 12% draw benefits in kind and use professional services and 15% combine benefits in kind and in cash	Social assumption of FC and legislative support for family ethic. Class differences in care – L / c less accepting of residential care. Decrease in assumption of caring for parents or partner. LTCI does not increase social solidarity. Desire by OP and state to increase this.
Greece	Yes in Constitution	Not enforceable in practice	No, minimal (6days) care leave for children and dependent OP (effectively state employees only)	No. Tax relief if co-resident and dependent	Social expectation to care without recognition of role
Hungary	Was obligatory between spouses and generations. Family Act 1952, 1986	LAs have care and financial responsibility for OP – regional variations	Ltd, less than 4hrs work p.d. can get nursing fee but low level. (may not be less than 60% of old age pension) Must pay pension contribution from this.	LA pays. No financial incentive to care. Low take up	Social expectation to care extends to wider society. But shift to more formal support for OP + new services. OP often mistrusts others including relatives. FC

Country	Legal Obligation	Legal Enforcement of Duties of FC	Rights of FC - pension, leave	Financial recognition	Role of FC and social attitudes
Ireland	None No state responsibility either	Irish Health Boards included the means of adult children in assessing eligibility of OP for financial support for the costs of nursing home care – now judged contrary to relevant statutory regulations.	Pension credits only available depending on receipt of Carers' Allowance. Inadequate coverage of costs, Carers Benefits taxable. Max. 139.7 €, p.w. 209.6 for 2. Eligible for return to Education allowance when caring responsibilities end. Respite grant. Carer's Charter	Tax based provisions for carers. Tax relief and medical expenses. Only 600 got Carers' Benefit (if takes time out from employment) – not everyone is eligible. Financial support most important issue for FCs. Carers Allowance means tested – 129.14 € p.w.	receiving nursing care fee often suspicious of formal services. Social expectation to care with increasing recognition of role. Changes with the rise of the 2 income family and rising employment levels. No inform on minorities and care.
Italy	Yes to the third degree; a family member requiring assistance, can ask for 'alimony' from the family[58], who may fulfil this obligation either by paying an amount of money each month or by accepting and supporting the person needing assistance in their own houses (articles 433, 438, 443 of	Article 570 of the Penal Code provides for the offence of "violation of the obligations of family assistance" for those who neglect subsistence to the relevant relatives, incapable of working, etc No case law quoted but de facto pressure on relatives to pay for admission to residential or	Some- especially in public sector, have right of continuous or split unpaid leave up to two years, this period of leave is not calculated either in the length of service or in the social-insurance scheme. Few in private sector use this right.	Not nationally. At LA level ltd. economic contributions for FC caring for dependent OP at home as cash care allowances based on need and income (the State care allowance is granted only on the basis of necessity, being non-means-tested). Regional variations e.g. special vouchers in Lom-	Assumption of FC but ideological system on the family is changing. Still caring in the family is considered as the best solution Privately paid home care keeps on growing due to the weakening of the care obligations of families and to a public system confined to play a residual role of

[58] These persons, identified by law, are in the order: spouse; legitimate, legitimized, natural or adopted children, and, if they are lacking, to the closest descendants; parents and, if they are missing, the closest ancestors even natural, and adopters; sons and daughters-in-law; father- and mother-in-law; brothers and sisters, German or half with the former having precedence over the latter.

Country	Legal Obligation	Legal Enforcement of Duties of FC	Rights of FC - pension, leave	Financial recognition	Role of FC and social attitudes
	the Civil Code).	hospital and social care.		bardy. Milan. 328 / 2000 a fiscal policy introduces tax concessions for families with special care burdens, to overcome the problem of care that is totally disbursed by public services, and to discourage irregular forms of care work + other tax deductible costs.	funder (i.e. of financing care), such that nowadays this represents the main source for obtaining care services, once the provision of family care is no longer possible. It is largely an informal market, which also exists because it evades public regulations, but is more or less explicitly supported by the state.
Luxembourg	No	No	Yes contributions to pension funds only.		High institutional provision. Emergence of new attitudes to support OP at home. Small country and proximity to family – assumed family support but no details on actual social attitudes to F.care. Development of respite care suggest increasing recognition of FCs. And their need for support.
Malta	Yes- non maintenance of parent deducted from future inheritance	Very rare	Not rights but de facto respite care	Carers pension'- 70 € + weekly – cohabiting, for very dependent. Means tested Social Assistance for females caring. Means tested. VAT relief on things used by carers.	Not formally recognized but family has priority in social policy and support services. Assumed it was female duty, new values, men help financially. 41% of those with carers pension are men. Changes in

Country	Legal Obligation	Legal Enforcement of Duties of FC	Rights of FC - pension, leave	Financial recognition	Role of FC and social attitudes
					women's roles, small families recognized as meaning difficulties for FCs.
Netherlands	NO – Govt. and public assumes it	No case law on the rights and obligations of FCs. Negotiation with needs assessment agency as to what is extra care for FC.	Many -Financing Career break (since 1998) offers the possibility for a palliative care leave. Since 2002 broadened, but compensation is low and e many rules and conditions that do not stimulate people to arrange this kind of care leave. Ministry support FCS thru' needs assessment, stimulation of voluntary work, crisis care, respite care, monitoring of the effect of informal care, financial aspects, combination of work and informal care, and raising more attention for informal care among professional caregivers.	Yes – 13% of FCs with extra expenses receive financial compensation, of which 73% from the care receiver. (Personal Care Budget) Only 6% from social security, 6% via taxes, and 20% mentioned an unknown source. On average the compensation was 285 € in 2001, Income tax measures	80% assume FC as a matter of course – though OP less. Recent changes in health care implicate FCs who are expected to provide more care for their relatives.
Norway	no legal obligations of caring between adult generations	No	Pension / credit rights - all carers are given pension points - 3 a year (corresponding to a wage clearly below average).	1,850 persons received a municipal care wage for care of OP – irrespective of income- but difficult to get, has to involve heavy duties and most FCs don't apply for it. But 30,132 persons aged 65+	'Welfare state orientation' = expectations about relative responsibilities of the welfare state and the family in the 3 domains of social policies and services for older people: financial support, instru-

Country	Legal Obligation	Legal Enforcement of Duties of FC	Rights of FC - pension, leave	Financial recognition	Role of FC and social attitudes
				received assistance pension from the National social security board in 2002 for those needing care due to long-term illness, injury or impairment.	mental help and personal care. A person's 'preferences for care' are a compromise between normative considerations and personal preferences
Poland	Yes, financial obligations (allows for family interdependence) –state obligations only to "families with difficult social and material situation" (defined) via LAs	Yes, also with joint legal agreement on inheritance in exchange for care.	Employed FCs of disabled (all ages) have the right to 2 / 52 leave (not self-employed)	Not to carer but "attendance allowance" for ALL > 75s	Social expectation to care without recognition of role
Portugal	Constitutional right after 1974 to social protection from state. In Civil Law Code descendants obliged by law to provide for their ascendants – social security policy operates when they cannot provide such care.	Civil rights to protect OP – right to sustenance under strong protection (Art. 2003) for sustenance, housing, clothing, Article 2009 No.1b also.	Public employees right to 15 days per year under the cover of 'family medical certification' to care for OP – but in private sector only available for care of those under 10 years.	No. Financial help only to dependent OP who may use it to pay FC	Reciprocity in families, Social expectation to care without recognition of role, Indirect state support e.g. day care centres, health centres. Social pressure accompanied by hostility towards institutions. Social change in attitudes with other pressures plus increased social provision. Gradual development of partnership between formal and informal carers.
Slovenia	Yes for adult children and step children if parents / stepparents cannot work	Policy and planning to support dependent OP being developed, includ-	7-14 days / year paid compensation for nursing sick co-habiting close	New Act for disabled (may include OP) to choose a "family assis-	1) See as for Czech above. 2) Also, parents substantially help young

Country	Legal Obligation	Legal Enforcement of Duties of FC	Rights of FC - pension, leave	Financial recognition	Role of FC and social attitudes
	and do not have sufficient funds for living. Financial obligation to support e.g. costs of residential care, but no legal obligation to care, although "unwritten rule" for at least temporary FC	ing home health care.	family members.	tant" (obligatory training) with partial payment for loss of work – applies to OP in certain cases, with criteria being defined. Attendance allowance paid to person (including dependent OP) needing constant care.	families – OP with property want to leave it to children and won't sell, but not always accompanied by reciprocity in care by children. People believe the State will take care of everything. "Society takes FC for granted and they do not exist as far as politicians are concerned."
Spain	Yes, Spanish civil regulations assign the responsibility for attending and caring for the dependent elder on the spouse and children (Spanish Civil Code. Book I). - spouses and all ascendants and descendants are reciprocally obliged to give maintenance proportionate to the means of the donor and the needs of the receiver.	Infringement to fulfil legal duties of assistance will be punished with arrest from eight to twenty weekends (Spanish Penal Code).	FC not recognized. ordinance. (Law 39 / 1999, Conciliation of family and working life) contemplates the right to a reduction in the working day with a proportional reduction of salary, and / or leave for a time not exceeding one year to look after a relative who, for reasons of age, is unable to look after him / herself.	40% of FC homes get under 600 € p.m. Regional Govts may give family subsidies. e.g. Aut.Com Madrid gives cash aid to FCs if annual income of the family is under 9,286 € and OP very disabled. The max. amount of aid is 2,710 € p.a. Tax reductions - by age and for expenses associated with the assistance of the elderly or disabled when the taxpayer is over 65	Expected and few services. Attention to FCs is very recent.
Sweden	No statutory responsibility for children to provide care or economic support for their family members	NO	Yes, Care Leave Act (1989) provides right to paid leave for those under 67 years and in the	Yes, plus the integration of carer support into the formal care management system Attendance al-	The re-discovery of FC following decades of expectations that the state will provide all necessary

Country	Legal Obligation	Legal Enforcement of Duties of FC	Rights of FC - pension, leave	Financial recognition	Role of FC and social attitudes
			labour force for up to 60 days to attend to a family member in a terminal care situation. Covered under National Social Insurance at the same level as sickness payment	lowance: an untaxed cash payment to the dependent, used to pay the family member for her help. The monthly payment is modest (SEK 5 000 / month (~ 550 €).	services for OP – Carer 300 project
Switzerland	Variations by Cantons				OP is funded and makes decisions. Assumption of FC with principle of subsidiarity, where the family, the individuals take their own responsibility in terms of care. The state intervenes only when the family cannot find any other alternative Policies are still to the importance of FC and have not really grasped the scope of the issue, neither in economic terms, neither in societal terms.
UK	No	No	N.I. Credit paid for every week FC gets Invalid Care Allowance (unless they elected to pay the lower 'married woman's stamp' some years ago). Or Home Responsibilities Protection for every complete year a FC cared for	Yes. Several wholly or partly means tested includes Carers Allowance, Invalid Care Allowance. FCs may claim £ 43.15 a week; Carer Premium, an additional sum of up to £ 25.80 a week paid as part of Income Support,	Individual decisions – depending on OP and family relations. No public assumption of FC though widespread.

Country	Legal Obligation	Legal Enforcement of Duties of FC	Rights of FC - pension, leave	Financial recognition	Role of FC and social attitudes
			someone provided they are getting Attendance Allowance or Disability Living Allowance care component at the middle or higher rate. This protects the state pension. Vouchers – issued by LA entitling FC to leave by paying for prof. Care. incentives to help carers get back to work. Some former FCs are entitled to Housing Benefit and Council Tax Benefit or Rate Rebate for 4 wks after they go back to work. Employers who take on former FCs can sometimes benefit from paying less N.I. at first. Additional Personal Tax allowance for married men with dependant children and whose wives are severely physically or mentally disabled throughout the tax year.	Income Based Job Seekers Allowance, Housing Benefit and Council Tax Benefit. From Oct 2002 people over 65 can make a claim for the carers' allowance, but if have pension the same or higher than the ICA rate will not get allowance but may be entitled to the Carers premium if they are on a low income. Direct Payments to FCs from Social services can only be spent on getting the support the carer has been assessed as needing.	

5.7 Annex 7 – Matrix Residential Care Services (Institutional care, includes residential homes, nursing homes, short and long term care hospitals)

Country	% in residential care (60+, 65+) Availability	Costs of residential care - Affordability	Family care contribution	Training of workers	Quality and control of residential care
Austria	**Residential care** – No growth 17% of all women aged 85+ use such care. 68,511 places in senior and nursing homes age 60 + in 740 institutions; about 49,800 "nursing" beds in old age and nursing homes and 18,004 places in residential care for less frail elderly; also old-age homes, have some nursing beds, thus distinction between old age and nursing homes impossible Approx. 40,000 women and 11,000 men in OP's homes or nursing homes; Proportions of OP unchanged since the 1960s and no major growth in institutional care expected. **Respite** – growth **Sheltered housing** - growth **Hospital stay – decline in length of stay** OP 60+ = 53%; 75+ = 26% of total stays in hospitals **Rehabilitation** – home service **Hospice – palliative care** – yes, new developments residential and at home. **Dementia** – move away from 'old' institu-	Yes - LTC Allowance. + up to 80% of pension used to finance public residential care. Dependent persons (defined by the criteria for long-term care benefits) have a legal right to admission to public residential care regardless of income. Most residents are beneficiaries of long-term care allowances.[59] Payment to the agency bearing the costs, usually the provincial authority. The balance is paid as pocket money. Insurance Funds handle 75% of the financing of care 39% of nursing home	NO. Carer doesn't pay Mainly unmarried and / or childless OP in homes. No tradition of cooperation between FC and staff	Lack of nation-wide regulations and standards. In particular, home helpers, geriatric aides and family helpers are trained on the basis of regional regulations. Additionally, there exist curricula developed by non-profit providers.	The provincial authorities are responsible for the construction, up-keep and operation of nursing homes and to guarantee minimum standards Ltd to ratio of clients / carers + complaints NGOs have internal controls This is desired by OP and FC

---

[59] For instance, in Lower Austria more than half of all residents are classified in long-term care level 4 or higher; only 6 % of all residents do not receive long-term care allowances (Löger, Amann, 2001: 67).

Country	% in residential care (60+, 65+) Availability	Costs of residential care - Affordability	Family care contribution	Training of workers	Quality and control of residential care
	tional care	expenditures are covered by contributions.			
Belgium	**Residential care** – 1,875 rest homes for 84,193 people with limited disabilities and 896 nursing homes for 28,670 people with major disabilities. Many rest homes and nursing homes have waiting lists, especially those nursing homes with wards for people suffering from dementia. Criteria for admission - Multi-disciplinary evaluation reports and standardized evaluation scales used for admission- strict criteria including need for help with ADL, inability to live at home. Some homes admit, others exclude people with dementia. Majority are private not for profit. **Respite care** within 122 centres in nursing homes in the Flemish Region. In Walloon Region, almost no respite care. **Sheltered housing – for dementia +?** **Hospital stay** geriatric ward beds decreased Rehabilitation? **Hospice – palliative care** **Dementia** – yes special wards, plus innovatory small units – cantous – see France.	Costs av. Monthly € 991.57. Higher than wages and difference growing. 35% rest homes / 45% nursing homes / 80% HC services and 100% home nursing financed by public – tax and social contributions, Fed. Govt compensates for dependent 65+ taking into account and household living in a point scale. Flemish – compensation for non medical costs.	Some will need help from relatives to finance their stay. May get benefits from the Public Centre for Social Work which can try to get reimbursement from the children of the person involved. – varies. In Flanders FC at home may be more expensive to FC than residential care.	Difficulties in finding certified nurses. Govt. ameliorating wages and working conditions.	Good quality.

Country	% in residential care (60+, 65+) Availability	Costs of residential care - Affordability	Family care contribution	Training of workers	Quality and control of residential care
Bulgaria	135 long term care facilities covering 11 078 OP. **Residential care** – *Homes for elderly people* accommodate those unable to look after themselves and satisfy their basic needs; persons who are certified with first or second degree of disability and active treatment in their case has ended; persons who have no relatives to take care of them; persons who have not signed a contract for ceding property against obligation for financial support and / or care. **Respite** **Sheltered housing** – NO **Hospital stay** **Rehabilitation** **Hospice – palliative care** – NO **Dementia**	Paid for from state and OP pension. A contract may be signed for ceding property against obligation for financial support and / or care.	No	Yes	?
Czech Republic	74 499 beds in total including 54 261 beds for adults. **Residential** – Long waiting lists, No long-term nursing care institutions. A quite high preference amongst OP for residential care. 67% of 60 years consider institutions to be a better solution and a better guarantee of care than living at home or in a sheltered home with home help. Criteria for admission to home or a boarding home for pensioners are: achievement of the retirement age and submission of the application for placement,	Free –OP continue to receive all of pension + any dependence allowance. Even for long-term stays of more than a year, covered by health care insurance. Health insurance companies try to limit the stay to 3 months in their individual contracts with facili-	Not financial – may even benefit from OP pension when in residential health care. Can pay extra for better facilities FCs try to compensate for poor nutrition and inadequate nursing. FCs usually support OP in sheltered units.	Skilled nursing personnel considered unnecessary in social residential institutions despite providing services for dependent and sick older people. Directors of residential homes do not need to meet any qualification criteria	Post 1989 NGOs developed many innovative types of care and services and have filled in many gaps. Residential homes originally owned by the state get regular funding from the state budget, NGOs have to raise their own funds and they have to apply for

Country	% in residential care (60+, 65+) Availability	Costs of residential care - Affordability	Family care contribution	Training of workers	Quality and control of residential care
	Respite – Res. Care used for temporary-respite care, but limited places and long waiting lists for placement especially in Prague and other cities **Sheltered housing** in smaller units in community Hospital stay limit the duration of a patient's stay in acute departments and OP often not welcome. **Rehabilitation** – no **Hospice – palliative care** – 6 hospices with 171 beds run by NGOs, new **Dementia** – yes, new	ties but families not able or willing to take care of the OP by-pass this 3 months limit by moving their OP from one facility to another (and from one insurance company to another).	For OP in standard old large facilities, they are often remote and FC can't get to them		a grant from the state budget. Grants are distributed through the process of public competition controlled by Ministry of Labour and Social Affairs (and by Ministry of Health). Applications have to be submitted each year
Denmark	**Residential** – Decline in nursing home beds from 31,000 in 1999 to 24,000 in 2003. 1987 ended construction of residential nursing homes and encouraged development of independent specialised housing for OP with care services being provided in the home. "Lost" nursing home places replaced by independent housing units for older people – their number has increased from 32,000 in 1999 (had been 18,000 in 1994) to almost 43,000 in 2003. All but 65 nursing home places out of almost 26,000 have the highest level of provision. **Respite** **Sheltered housing** –Sheltered housing units has also declined– from 4640 in 1999to 3572 in 2003.	Rent accommodation.	Good / Innovative practice - authorities are obliged to establish a relatives' council – the aim is to improve dialogue and involvement of relatives of residents	Yes	Yes Accountability with regard to the quality of care is with LA even when recipients of care may choose a provider other than the public provider. In addition, a framework of mechanisms, which allow the recipient (or relatives) to complain and appeal, is in place.

Country	% in residential care (60+, 65+) Availability	Costs of residential care - Affordability	Family care contribution	Training of workers	Quality and control of residential care
	Units for OP increased 88,000 in 1999 to 91,000 in 2003. 48,000 of this total are linked to extensive care services. **Hospital stay / Rehabilitation** **Hospice – palliative care** **Dementia** – In 2002, there were almost 5000 places designated specifically for persons suffering from dementia – increasing steadily				
Finland	**Residential** – In 2001 3.7% of persons aged 65+ and 8% aged 75+ were living in old age homes or housing with 24 hours assistance. 89% on inst care. 529 mill € on inst care. 11% by organizations, and less than 1% by small enterprises. **Respite** – acute, short-term or interval. Care in institutions Sheltered housing=Service housing **Hospital stay** – the number of clients aged 65+ is decreasing in all institutional care in health care. **Rehabilitation** - yes **Hospice – palliative care**- yes, some run by private foundations, most in health centre hospitals. – or at home. **Dementia**– in 1995 (latest data) from 100 000 demented persons 40 000 were in long term residential care.	Service housing 24 hr assistance – 37 e daily bed charge Residential home – 96,9 e, Inpatient primary HC – 135,9 e. Need for institutional care declined because of increase in functional capacity of 65+	Depends on client's financial standing and may not exceed 80% net income monthly. (must have at least 80 e for own expenses) Spouse situation also taken into account for LTC	Good / Innovative practice Yes Professional certification defined by legislation – only qualified workers can get a job. High level of geriatric knowledge among professionals.	Ministry of social Affairs and Health gives national recommendations for the dev. and quality of services for OP – HC, service housing and residential care. Act as guidelines for Municipalities to evaluate the services they offer. Association of Fin. L and Reg Auth has also tried to improve Quality of care – but each chooses own methods. Good / Innovative practice - Common repeat use of questionnaire on client's opinions on availability, adequacy and

Country	% in residential care (60+, 65+) Availability	Costs of residential care - Affordability	Family care contribution	Training of workers	Quality and control of residential care
					functionality of services i.e. user feedback.
France	**Residential** – 471,000 persons > 60 years; most state, some private. 6.500 traditional homes for OP (public, private non profit and commercial): av. no. of places (1996): 60 in private non profit institutions, 75 in public homes, 86 in public homes in public hospitals, 48 in private commercial homes. Population mainly female (widows, 62%, 29% singles and divorced). Pop. old due to the av. age when entering: end of 1999, 79 years for men, and 84 years for women. **Respite.** Some institutions specialize in short term care and very helpful to FCs. **Sheltered housing** – 3.000 beds **Hospital stay** 1,100 nursing homes, generally depending on a public hospital; **Rehabilitation** **Hospice - palliative care** **Dementia** 1975, special institution developed for OP suffering from dementia: the *"Cantou"*. Twelve persons are living together;	Costs partly born by residents and regional governments (*Conseils généraux*) Enormous differences from one *département* to the other; costs: estimated at 3.9 billion in 2003 and 4 billion in 2004. The average monthly rate is 1,300 € (2004), the average income of pensioners 1,440 / month for men and 894 / month for women	No – institutions run like hospitals. FC limited to visiting – often reluctantly. Social integration *extra muros* is passive. 70% report regular family contact and visits from friends, former neighbours and colleagues. Amongst those (30%) who do not have any contact with their family two in three declare that they do not have children or that all family members are dead But in CANTOU family members are invited to spend as much time as possible within the group, participating in and generating all sorts of indoor and outdoor activities.	Training available- but no advantage in many contexts.	New law to up date and improve the 30,000 medico-social institutions for old and disabled persons (residential and domiciliary services), includes the obligation of quality evaluation. But since the new government, "Raffarin III", (March 2004), this intention seems to have lost its priority. Very negative images as old hospices for indigent / problematic and were huge. Reality is better but image stops FCs wanting to use residential homes. 15% of residential insts need total restoration, 30% partly, i.e. 200,000 beds, 1 / 3 of total;

Country	% in residential care (60+, 65+) Availability	Costs of residential care - Affordability	Family care contribution	Training of workers	Quality and control of residential care
Germany	**Residential** – Growth in nos. + suffering from dementia. In 1999 8,659 LTC = 645,456 places. > half (56,6%) financed by independent charitable organisations, 1 / 3 by private commercial bodies (34,9%) and the rest public (8,5%). 28% (554,000) of people in need of care are in residential care. Older generally than those cared for in domestic setting. 66% in residential care are 80 years+ but only 44% of cared for in domestic setting are > 80 **Respite** – some available and paid for by LTCI but urban / rural differences. **Sheltered housing** – many kinds **Hospital stay** –increase in geriatric in patient facilities though long term trend is to reduce length of stay to reduce costs. **Rehabilitation** – yes **Hospice - palliative care** – yes in all forms **Dementia** In 2002, there were almost 5000 places designated for persons suffering from dementia –increasing steadily	LTC insurance can be used to pay towards care costs. Care allowances calculated according to the care categories which pay for medical treatment care and social care. Other costs paid for by the person in need of care, with pension and savings or by reverting to the resources of close family members. If OP or relatives have no resources the social welfare pays in accordance with the Federal Law on Welfare Benefits "support in difficult life-situations". In 1998 36% of all residents of old peoples homes were dependent on social welfare. All pay some contribution to H and SC.	No- FCs seen as disruptive- not consulted in hospital care, just provide clean laundry, contact and support,	At least 50% of the nursing care staff employed in residential institutions must have a professional qualification if they care for more than 4 persons in need of care and if special care interventions are necessary	Yes- LTCI thru' regulations for professional service providers that lay down the content of services offered, organizational modes and the required qualifications for carers / nurses no standardized quality control procedures for sheltered housing and t the quality varies greatly
Greece	**Residential-** Estimate less than 1% of 65+. NGOs, Churches, Foundations and private homes – but no adequate break-	Min. in illegal, crowded facilities 600 €, av. 1000 –	If OP has inadequate income, families pay. When in hospital FCs	Training requirements for head nurses but not for assistants. No	Ministry has an Inspectorate but focus traditionally on envi-

Country	% in residential care (60+, 65+) Availability	Costs of residential care - Affordability	Family care contribution	Training of workers	Quality and control of residential care
	down of numbers in each kind. Exact nos. unknown since many places not registered. Traditionally had to be self-caring but increasing numbers are dependent on entry and many now effectively nursing homes. In a non represent study of those with a FC 17% of the men and 29% of the women being cared for spent their terminal phase in a nursing home or clinic **Private clinics** – numbers no known. **Sheltered housing** – no **Hospital stay** – decreasing length of stay for OP **Rehabilitation** – 3 public + private units. High demand, inadequate coverage, no home rehab service, although some insurance cover for limited physiotherapy at home. **Hospice – palliative care** – for cancer patients **Dementia** - recent development of respite care and FC support by Alzheimer groups	1400 single rooms, best residential homes approx 2000 € - cost depends on the degree of dependency. IKA pensions are approximately 500 € p.m.. Only in exceptional cases will the Insurance Funds pay the full costs. Private clinics – Insurance funds will pay for many of costs for terminally ill patients,	have to offer practical help in nursing. Small residential homes in local areas, including religious homes, also used by working family carers when can't accommodate the OP with them- FC who are proximate often provide personal care, food and company for the OP when the carer is not at work. Most residential homes encourage the active participation of family carers as it both eases the care tasks for the staff and improves the well-being of the older person.	minimum numbers of staffing for homes.	ronment and space standards rather than quality of care. Families often very concerned with level and quality of care. Private clinics registered with Ministry and have basic levels of medical and nursing staff, although for very intensive care needs, it is often still necessary to employ private nursing assistants as in state hospitals et e
Hungary	**Residential** 3.2% over 60. In 1993 28 742 persons over 60. In 2001 was 41% higher). Unmet needs-. In 2000 11 767 persons were on the waiting list for places, and 53% waiting > a year Foundations, churches, private businesses Institutions may set other criteria, e.g. age. New residential home, younger older per-	in rehabilitation institutions the fee charged may not exceed 80% of income of the recipient of care Private or NGO institutions which do not	Not financial In hospitals FCs have to help because of nursing shortages. Costs of paying for better medicines, toilet needs, better meals.	Has begun	Qualitative development can also be observed in the case of residential homes, especially in the wake of investigations by the ombudsman and as a result of further

Country	% In residential care (60+, 65+) Availability	Costs of residential care - Affordability	Family care contribution	Training of workers	Quality and control of residential care
	sons, built by foundations and churches are of a high standard (in contrast to rooms for 4-16 persons in the state home) and provide good services. – With mortality rate dropping and institutions' "turnover speed" reduced. Consequently they were forced to raise the age for entry (e.g. to 70 or 75 years) and also the sum to be paid on entry. **Respite** Used for respite care especially by urban OP. **Sheltered housing** **Hospital stay** – frequent early discharge because of high costs **Rehabilitation** – some, inadequate **Hospice – palliative care** – yes **Dementia**	wish to receive the state per capita funding are free to set an entry charge usually amounting to several million HUF (or the transfer of an apartment they are able to sell), as well as a monthly fee for the care.= 1%			training for the staff, but the standard of care depended to a large extent on the maintaining body, the age of the institution and the attitude of its head.
Ireland	**Residential** – Ltd public and mainly private 6.196 beds in private and voluntary homes with public finance support + 1,281 contract beds with contract of health board with private sector as private care. Plus 385 further beds. 80% of all beds get public funding. 4775 beds in private and voluntary homes 90-95% occupancy rates. Maj over 75, only 16% aged 65-75 **Sheltered housing** - yes **Hospital stay**	Means tested, client or family may pay costs Nursing home care is means tested. Tax relief allowed to client or family.	Some supervision. Liaison with care staff.	The majority of employed staff are professionally qualified. Specialist training is available for palliative care and dementia care. Training in nursing staff and care staff is compulsory	There is no national nursing home inspectorate at the moment, although plans for a nursing home inspectorate are being made and legislation is being drafted (2005). Private nursing homes must be registered with the HSE and are required to meet certain standards. However, in-

Country	% in residential care (60+, 65+) Availability	Costs of residential care - Affordability	Family care contribution	Training of workers	Quality and control of residential care
	Rehabilitation - yes **Hospice - palliative care** – yes 6 centres, 7 specialists + specialist palliative care teams and supported by NGOs **Dementia** is under the remit of Psychiatry of Old Age services provided by the Health Service Executive. Provided on inand out patient basis in non-acute hospitals. Psychiatry of Old Age services also available in the community, although suffers from staff shortages. Voluntary organisations also provide dementia services such as day care, home care, and respite care.				spection staff are over-stretched and under-funded and care standards can vary. The Irish Hospice Foundation has published standards for palliative and bereavement care.
Italy	**Residential** 2% of 65+ in homes. Bed vacancies in nursing homes, ranging from 34 per 1000 inhabitants in the North, to 13 in Central Italy, and down to 10 in the South. Of all OP cared for in residential settings, 73% live in the North, 15% in Central Italy and 12% in the South 38% of residential facilities for OP are public, 58% are private and the remaining 4% are mixed structures, with relevant differences between social–assistance and health–care structures, where not for - profit institutions have a 42% and 25.8% presence, respectively OP more dependent in all institutions. **Respite** – some **Sheltered housing** – social housing gradually becomes more used by higher	The family costs for private care at home are often lower than the residential fees Only 5% of elderly people who make use of services offered by residential care do not pay anything, whilst expenses for 62% of residents fall entirely upon the family, whereas in 33% of cases health care costs are partially covered by the National Health System fund.	Families of 35–40% of the residents probably contribute equivalent to 250-500 € p.m... Especially in S. Italy and for severely affected OP relatives often required both in hospitals and in many residential homes to provide night assistance and personal care. FC support may be the condition sine qua non for a OP's admission to the caring facility but has positive aspects to ensure	Yes – but though in law difficulties in getting all staff trained because of shortages.	Residential homes designed for self-sufficient elderly people are improperly transformed into long care hospital centres

Country	% in residential care (60+, 65+) Availability	Costs of residential care - Affordability	Family care contribution	Training of workers	Quality and control of residential care
	dependent. **Hospital stay – 1 / 3** of beds for severely ill people occupied by > 65 patients Av. period of stay is shorter in public V private structures = 27 days V 91 days. **Rehabilitation** – yes **Hospice – palliative care** **Dementia** NGO led project initiatives		non abandonment		
Luxembourg	**Residential** - 4328 beds in 35 integrated centers and 14 nursing homes. i.e. 63,140 aged 65+ = 6.8% - (higher than neighbouring countries which have 4%) One of highest levels of availability in EU. Expanding by 1350 units. **Respite** – yes **Sheltered housing** – esp. for mental disabled have started Integrated Centre for Older People with Disabilities opened, with capacity for 56 senior residents, managed by the "Fondation Kraizbierg". **Hospital stay** **Rehabilitation** - yes **Hospice- palliative care** yes, available and special training courses for staff in palliative care available from Min. of Health. **Dementia**	35.82. € per hour versus 48 € for home care High incomes mean most people can afford it. And Nat Fund of Solidarity pays any additional costs if someone can't afford full costs. (700 beneficiaries) But adequately funded and staff well paid	No. Funding is to OP through the National Solidarity Fund	More than half are foreign workers (mainly EU) in the care and social sector. Yes – if not already qualified, professional training for assistant nurses available. Special courses in palliative care available from Min. of Health. Each employer in the social sector has to guarantee 20 hours of advanced training – thus continuous training is compulsory	Yes – A Quality management system being developed.
Malta	**Residential** > 5% of OP 65+ live in government and private run homes, but demand increasing.	Private rates are higher than those in State owned or	Good care but FCs important in providing psychological sup-	The majority of employed staff are professionally qualified.	Mainly standards of accommodation, cleanliness etc.

Country	% in residential care (60+, 65+) Availability	Costs of residential care - Affordability	Family care contribution	Training of workers	Quality and control of residential care
	Private homes (10) 2 of the 7 State-owned residential homes administered privately. 18 Church-run residential homes providing around 600 beds. Assessment Rehabilitation Team (ARTeam) decides on eligibility and priority of cases. To enter one of these homes, an elderly person must be fully mobile and capable of living independently. With one exception, these homes do not have a nursing wing. A dependent OP goes to a place where nursing facilities are available, such as SVPR or one of the private homes. **Respite** Resl. Homes used also for Respite care. **Sheltered housing** **Hospital stay** **Rehabilitation** – Yes **Hospice** – palliative care **Dementia**	Church run residential homes depending on levels of 'hotel' accommodation and nursing services required. Costs 18 to 46 € daily. In the largest state institution with more than 1000 beds resident pays 80% of his total income but must still have 1380 € p.a. for self. In other homes the OP pays 60% of his total income, with same condition. Estimated actual daily cost per resident amounts to € 48.30 – subsidized by State. Less nuns means higher use of lay professionals and as a result costs are rising	port, acting as intermediaries, providers of information, Also mundane caring tasks for the OP e.g. as washing their clothes, personal care, cooking meals, housekeeping, accompanying the patient to appointments, and taking specimens and collecting results.	The others, mainly those offering 'hotel type' services receive in-house training	
Netherlands	**Residential** 5% of OP live in residential homes, and about 2,5% in nursing homes **Respite** - yes **Sheltered housing** **Hospital stay** 12% aged 65- 74 admitted; 13% 75 + V age 55-64 (7%) and 35- 54	Income related Low co-payment (*max.* € 685.40 p.m.), High co-payment (*max.* € 1,700.- p.m.)	1 in 10 FC give care to people living in health care facilities or special housing facilities (financial affairs, groceries, transport, washing /	Residential homes have low level of trained staff Nursing homes for dependent have trained staff	Large service organizations have own controls, but small organizations do not.

Country	% in residential care (60+, 65+) Availability	Costs of residential care - Affordability	Family care contribution	Training of workers	Quality and control of residential care
	(5%). 25% 75 years + contacted a medical specialist **Rehabilitation** Res. Homes used for rehabilitation of both elderly and younger patients, and in diagnosis and functional assessment. **Hospice - palliative care** – yes available. **Dementia**		bathing, (un-dressing, feeding). In holiday periods some nursing and residential homes ask for extra help from FCs because of personnel shortages		
Norway	**Residential** 9 / 10 older parents prefer a residential setting if they can no longer live by themselves. Many units and sheltered housing - 5.2% of total 67+ in sheltered housing (15.1% by age 90), 6.6 all aged 67+, by age 90+ was 38.5%. Increase in sheltered housing and decrease in nursing homes. Shortage of beds has declined. **Admission** – is degree of dependency. **Sheltered housing** 2000 / 2001, 80% LAs had special units with sheltered living for persons with dementia, (V 70% 1996) LAs without such units are small (less than 2500 inhabitants) **Respite** 55% of LAs had special respite arrangements for persons with dementia. **Hospital stay** – earlier release **Rehabilitation** – everywhere but a bed shortage **Hospice – palliative care** **Good / Innovative practice** -2 LAs have	Payment relates to OP income = 75% of baseline of the National S.I. € 6,600, supplemented with maximum 85% of other forms of income (if any), after taxes. There is a basic exemption of € 730. On average, users pay about one third of the total costs for nursing home. Low income residents pay less Total costs vary between municipalities. (€ 54.900) in 2004. Irrespective of income and costs, every resident is guaranteed a minimum amount at own, free disposal, about € 250 p.m.	Good / Innovative practice - FCs free to develop their "caregiver careers" in the institutional setting. E.g. spouses, visit partners as a part of their daily routines give personal care and assist at meals. As an ideal, staff and FCs have initial and follow-up meetings to clarify expectations and consider the involvement of the FC. In principle, it is up to the family caregiver to decide how much care they want to give and the extent to which they keep on to the relationship.	Lack of trained nursing and care personnel.	Action Plan has focused on modernising nursing homes + with single rooms for all OP. LAs responsible for quality and standards of primary health and social services, regardless of who carries out the services, cpr. supervision legislation. Control and supervision are shared between the offices of the County governor and the County physician

Country	% In residential care (60+, 65+) Availability	Costs of residential care - Affordability	Family care contribution	Training of workers	Quality and control of residential care
	organized LTC in institutions built in Spain, as part of their regular old age care services				
Poland	**Residential** – 78,935 people including 10.114 bedridden; 23.6% aged 61-74 and 29.8% aged 75 and more. Despite increase in places may waiting to be admitted. 811 homes 21.1 places per 10 thousand people. This has increased by 3.3 places since 1990. 18.6 to 23.9 per 10,000 people post-production age. V. uneven regional distribution though more elderly also has more institutions. **Ex mural activities** for other OP e.g. meal, therapeutic activities similar to the day care centres. **Respite** – no **Sheltered housing** – No sheltered housing **Hospital stay** **Rehabilitation** **Hospice – palliative care**	The cost of stay covered by the inhabitant's own pension (3 / 4 of the pension) and by their families, but since this rarely covers costs mainly by social care funds. 75% homes financed by LAs and managed by them. Other institutions are managed by church and NGOs. Over 130 private care homes have a total of 2300 places- these vary in price and are more expensive. LAs admit based on criteria (medical plus loss of fitness (need for nursing care) or decline in social conditions (loneliness, lack of family, lack of ability to manage the household, very low income etc.)	Yes to costs if they can afford it. – Just 1%. FCs do not care in the institution or in a hospital – conflicts with prof. staff.	Yes	Varied but improving standard. Privately owned homes for the aged are not under supervision of social policy officers (there are documented cases of extreme neglect in the privately owned homes). Care institutions organised by NGOs are usually supervised by local social centres.
Portugal	**Residential** 1,550 residential homes and OP homes with 95.8% utilization / 50,607	Mainly private, Some not for profit financed	Not active or partnership, but institution	No. Heads of institutions	Current transformation into intensive

Country	% in residential care (60+, 65+) Availability	Costs of residential care - Affordability	Family care contribution	Training of workers	Quality and control of residential care
	65+, more women at all ages. 3.3% of pop. 848 OP Homes, 56 Residential homes. 28,802 on waiting list in 1993 Sheltered housing yes, with current transformation of Residential Homes **Hospital stay** Rehabilitation very few services: 17-27% of aged over 55, had access to rehabilitation. **Hospice – palliative care** **Dementia** – no	by state. Pref. for single elderly with low income and without FC in Old People's Homes Private OP Homes are v. expensive.	ask FC to participate in outings, festivals.	are qualified. Encouragement of training thru programme of Integrated support for the Elderly.	nursing homes or sheltered housing. Grandparent Plan under development to develop measures for the certification of institutional quality.
Slovenia	**Residential** 52 state homes. 4.3% of OP = 12,000. OP homes are full and long waiting periods. 1 / 4 of cared-for people at these homes die each year. Increasingly places with v. dependent needing health care. Av capacity around 200 beds; lowest 60 beds; av. rooms have 1.97 beds Some private homes with concession (8) residences. **Respite** - New facilities are hotels for the elderly, where OP live mostly temporarily and transitionally. They give FCs the chance to take a temporary break since no proper respite care. Temporary admission' only available in 2 public sector OP homes and in hospitals. **Sheltered housing** – new – 300 units in 9 places (studio and one-room apartments, some 2-room apartments.) High interest	Private- has to be paid for. Entitlement OP > 65 with mental / physical problems. The number of recipients of these services depends on their health conditions. Cared-for people pay for services themselves if they are financially capable. 2 / 3 OP in homes entirely covered the costs of care from own resources and with the help of relatives (out-of-pocket payers), 27.5% of	Earlier release from hospitals – where FC do not play any supporting part – and absence of rehab facilities means FCs faced by problems of care. FCs encouraged to work with Residential home – and more homes work as trainers / information for FCs of OP in home and in community.	Yes, institutional care is provided by trained personnel: social workers, trained nurses, occupational therapists, physiotherapists- they have finished specialized education / training. However these institutions also employ untrained personnel: sometimes unemployed people are offered work in institutions for a limited period e.g. a year. This is a programme to reduce unemployment, training in care	Yes- homes are of a high standard except for Human aspects – but they are also well controlled- A lot of out work with three-member control commissions, appointed by the Minister from the list of experts, perform regular and irregular professional and administrative controls. The list of 45 experts, who are additionally trained for control work, is proposed by the Social Chamber

Country	% in residential care (60+, 65+) Availability	Costs of residential care - Affordability	Family care contribution	Training of workers	Quality and control of residential care
	but in reality they are occupied relatively slowly because of high prices, inappropriate locations and, above all, the fact that people will not sell their home in old age and move into a smaller apartment **Hospital stay** – declining **Rehabilitation** - inadequate **Hospice – palliative care** **Dementia**	them needed help in the form of a co-payment and only 8% of people had the costs of care entirely paid. If OP not able to pay, adult children in the first place or municipalities in the second place are lawfully obliged to help them. People must pay for hotel services fully and their prices are higher than for homes of the public network. Temp admission – prices paid by OP / FC		available but not obligatory, and thus not implemented everywhere. They do basic hygiene care.	of Slovenia.

Country	% in residential care (60+, 65+) Availability	Costs of residential care - Affordability	Family care contribution	Training of workers	Quality and control of residential care
Spain	**Residential** The ratio of residential places was 3.4% of the over 65s, of which 1.26% were public- large increase. The ratio of public housing under care was 0.05% of the over 65s., Large Regional differences- with Catalonia as leader. Living alone, regardless of the existence of children, and serious dependency facilitate access **Sheltered housing** Also 4,280 guarded housing places in the country distributed around 396 houses. **Respite** temporary stays was 0.03% in 1999, almost entirely on the community of Madrid (0.17%) and in the Basque Country (0.09%) **Hospital stay** **Rehabilitation** **Hospice – palliative care** – essentially not available. **Dementia** - no	Public -.requires high dependency and little wealth Private - exclusively financial. 58.8% places financed wholly by the user, and the rest this by the public sector. 70% of the public cost for LTC is for residential services. User's contribution to the cost of the public residential places lies at around 75% of their pension. In 2000, private monthly price almost 900 €. But differences between profit-making institutions (some 1052 € p.m.) and the rest, normally religious, charging around half of the others. Public residences in 2000 were 702 €. Av. Price = 42% of highest average salary and 63% of the lowest average salary	Yes in hospitals- help to maintain hygiene, moral support and general supervision of their needs.	For higher level staff it exists	Mainly by Regions using administrative criteria - structural (location, internal distribution, facilities, services, etc.) and functional (internal regulations, prices, fire prevention, programming).
Sweden	**Residential / Sheltered housing** – Under	3 types of cost: hous-	Not expected though	50% care personnel	Yes municipality and

Country	% in residential care (60+, 65+) Availability	Costs of residential care - Affordability	Family care contribution	Training of workers	Quality and control of residential care
	one "umbrella" heading; "special housing" with service and care for OP comprising: nursing homes, OA homes, service houses, group homes Until early '80s, institutional care expanded with changes in population. But since stagnated. In 2003, 110 900 persons living in different forms of institutional care or in "special housing" for OP = service coverage of 7.2% of 65 yrs+ and 19% among those 80 yrs+.

Just 13% of OP in private care.

Hospital stay - Earlier discharges from hospital means OP are more frail when going into other forms of sheltered housing or going home.

Rehabilitation – thru' PHC

Hospice – palliative care – Palliative care available throughout the country.

Dementia – 25 000 beds in group homes | ing, meals, and care. Av. net-income among OP is 8 500 SEK p.m.. The average cost for housing is estimated to 2 500 SEK, food / meals to 2 400 SEK and cost for care at 500 SEK p.m.. On av. 5 400 SEK care p.m. or almost two thirds of income process of needs assessment, carried out by the municipal care manager. Access criteria may and do very much differ from one municipality to another. However, the level of dependency and degree of cognitive impairment is often decisive.

Innovative aspects - Admission is not based on means-testing. | families do participate. In recent years there is a shift in attitudes and care personnel are more and more focusing on the (former) carer, to collaborate and create *"carer- friendly institutions.* | has at present the requested training for the work (upper secondary school-level), primarily due to difficulties to recruit care personnel with adequate training and skills | national boards. The monitoring authorities work from the regional level. |
| Switzerland | **Residential** 1422 homes, corresponding to 76,024 Two thirds of the institutions are financed by public funds, one-third by private foundations. | | | Inadequate staffing – migrant workers resorted | |

Country	% in residential care (60+, 65+) Availability	Costs of residential care - Affordability	Family care contribution	Training of workers	Quality and control of residential care
	Respite – yes – in hospitals and some cantons have hostels **Sheltered housing** – no data **Hospital stay** **Rehabilitation** **Hospice – palliative care** **Dementia** – not in institutions				
UK	**Residential-** Between 2000 and 2001 a 3% decrease in residential care homes and a decrease of 3% in nursing homes and private hospitals and clinics. Over half (54%) of supported residents were in independent residential care homes, 27% were in independent nursing homes and 16% were in Local authority staffed homes. Maj over 85+ There were 431,200 residential places in 24,100 residential care homes and 186,800 registered beds in 5,700 nursing homes and private hospitals and clinics. **Respite** –widespread **Sheltered housing**- 3.5% of people aged 65 to 69 to 19% aged 85 **Hospital stay** **Rehabilitation** – full and specialised services in hospitals, day care and home care teams. Danger of ignoring the most frail, **Hospice – palliative care** – growth, NGOs	Average cost for private residential care was £302 per week and the average cost for private nursing care was £422 per week.– OAP is £80 per week. Majority of the funding for the care of older people is provided by the public sector. OP assets pay for residential costs (only £12000 pounds left) If individuals have more than £19,500 in capital then they have to pay the full cost of residential or nursing home care.	No	In house training for lower grade workers – professionals fully qualified. Overall low level of training for care workers, with training focusing on minimal health and safety requirements, not philosophy of care and the development of interpersonal skills. New requirement for 50% of care assistants to have NVQ Level 2 by 2005, providing a significant challenge for care homes	Nursing homes and care homes have to be inspected a minimum of twice a year. One inspection is announced so the homes are aware when they are coming, but one is unannounced workers know they are coming but inspection is that the inspectors turn up unannounced. The Care Standards Act has now set national standards so that services should be equivalent in different parts of the country. Inspection reports are publicly available.

Country	% in residential care (60+, 65+) Availability	Costs of residential care - Affordability	Family care contri- bution	Training of workers	Quality and control of residential care
	Dementia 1.5 million of people over 85.?				

5.8 Annex 8 – Matrix of Home Based Services

Countries	Availability of Home Based services Home Help and Local coordination centres; Day Care centres; Public sector; Home Health care – Dementia services; Respite care in the home	Additional comments	Costs of using service care Affordability	Quality & control of service – ISO. Training of Workers
Austria	**Home Help and Local coordination centres** 5% aged 65 + get home care. 17% among care dependent elderly – growth slowed post 1990's in nos. of clients and service hours. Few private services **Day Care centres** – Yes, growth. **Home health care** -Partial coverage **Dementia services** – yes and growing* - high demand. Inadequate coverage. **Respite care at home** - in some regions Services used by 60% of persons living alone and 41% of persons sharing a household.	Large regional disparities in organizational form, quality, development and co-ordination of services. HH usually 2 x week; in critical cases 5 x week or daily. Lower Austria 200+ Social Stations run by 4 NGOs as one-stop-shops offering services with home nursing and HH core competencies, + some respite care. NGOs provide 90% of community and semi-institutional care services; reimbursed by the province or LA.	With introduction of LTC Allowance about 1 / 3 persons receiving this cash payment is able to use more community services than before 27% of total expenditures for health and social services is covered by contributions of users and their relatives	**Inadequate quality control.** Control based on clients or family members' complaints, periodic home visits, and telephone contact with beneficiaries. "Structural quality assessment" used administratively e.g. client / carer ratio etc. NGOs have internal quality assurance programmes but unknown results. **Training**- Adequate- Most trained Regional standards. No nationwide regulations / standards for home & family helpers, geriatric aides.
Belgium	**Home Help and Local coordination centres** 4.9% of people 65-74 and 26.1% of 75 years + used home help in 2001. 136 local service centres- Flemish, access to professional care and information. 53 coordination centres in Walloon area. Demand exceeding provision.		Means tested with reductions for heavily dependent. Priority to OP with high dependency and low income. Costs for the OP relate to family income Min. € 0.50 p.h., max. real cost of help i.e. € 22.50 p.h. av. Contribution € 3 per hour, 30% higher if help needed 8 pm-7 am or Sats.; 60% higher	**Adequate quality control.** in Flanders must have mission statement. **Training**- Good. All trained certificates compulsory. H & SC workers being trained to work with FC

Countries	Availability of Home Based services Home Help and Local coordination centres; Day Care centres; Public sector; Home Health care – Dementia services; Respite care in the home	Additional comments	Costs of using service care Affordability	Quality & control of service – ISO. Training of Workers
	Day Care centres – Yes, growth. 0.3% of OP 65-74 years of age and 0.7% of OP 75 years + in 2001 **Home health care** - Comprehensive coverage **Dementia services** – yes and growing **Respite care** 10,000 hours of sit-in care p.a., at least half provided by volunteers.		on Sundays and public holidays. Very dependent get discounts.	
Bulgaria	**Home Help and Local coordination centres** 262 FC service offices with 35 172 places. **Day Care centres** – Yes, growth; provide possibility for day nursing including OP. **Home health care** -Partial coverage – integrated care with SS. **Dementia services** – yes in day care centres **Respite care**- no though summer camps offer some relief.	Social care includes bureaux for social services, homes for elderly people and clubs of the disabled. Soup kitchens provide food for indigent persons and families	Often difficult for people to pay the fees. social assistance benefits do not cover costs.	**Inadequate quality control.** Service dominated by quantitative indicators **Training** – Good virtually all.
Czech Republic	**Home Help and Local coordination centres** approx. 10% uses domiciliary services. 31% of communities covered by HH service- 107 000 clients. 26% lived in sheltered houses, 37% got meals on wheels, 24% visited personal hygiene centres, 13% used laundry	20% of 60+ have serious health problems Bigger LAs, establish houses of nursing care. 1879 nurses mostly organised in private or not for profit home care	GPs has a budget permitting home care but expensive for their budgets and agencies are able to provide nursing care on weekends and at nights. And thus less prescribed than hospital care – which does not come out of	**Inadequate quality control** – some HH service providers have own standards of quality. Ministry elaborated recommendations for general social care standards of quality. **Training**- Inadequate – many

Countries	Availability of Home Based services Home Help and Local coordination centres; Day Care centres; Public sector; Home Health care – Dementia services; Respite care in the home	Additional comments	Costs of using service care Affordability	Quality & control of service – ISO. Training of Workers
	services Private services also available. **Day Care centres** – Some day and week centres - 0,6% visited day centres for OP Large demand. **Home health care** -Partial coverage **Dementia services** – Yes – some for FCs thru' Alzheimer Associations. **Respite care**- Alzheimer linked FC only. Other services not available in home.	agencies.	their budget Growth in private payment for some HS. e.g. physiotherapists	untrained. No system of certification. Czech Association of Nurses introduced the system of registration and continual education of nurses but not compulsory
Denmark	**Home Help and Local coordination centres** 15% 60+ get HH, Of 700,000 67+, 172,000 67+ had LT HH, + 8-7000 67+ receive short-term HH. 50% 80+ get LT HH., 80% for personal care, 20% practical help in the home (cleaning, shopping and laundry).. 60% to 80+ Growth of private services **Day Care centres** - yes Home health care - comprehensive **Dementia services** – incomplete. DaneAge run volunteer-based respite service for FCs, **Respite care** – LA obliged under SS Law to provide FCs caring f / t with it.	50% of recipients get < 2 hours per week, av. hours per week is 4.5 under 80 and 6.1 for 80+. 13,000 recipients 67+ < 20 hrs p.w. 1,080,000 hours of HH weekly 100,000 persons suffer from dementia	Free, though many OP feel they should contribute to LA. Everyone eligible after a certain age. 12% 60+ buy in private home help services in the home while an additional 3% receive both public home-help services **and** buy in private services	**Adequate quality control –** Local government research institute (AKF) carries out evaluation and monitoring of services in LAs **Training** – Good, all trained DaneAge trains volunteers

Countries	Availability of Home Based services Home Help and Local coordination centres; Day Care centres; Public sector; Home Health care – Dementia services; Respite care in the home	Additional comments	Costs of using service care Affordability	Quality & control of service – ISO. Training of Workers
Finland	**Home Help** and **Local coordination centres** 10.6% age 65+ get HH- 4 / 5 from LAs, rest from private services. Personal care and service plans made by multi prof (H+SS) teams for persons in continuous need for care. Increased focus on older OP. Slight decline in numbers receiving HH and Home nursing. **Day Care centres** - yes public and private increasing **Home health care** - comprehensive **Dementia services** - Yes **Respite care** – yes- NGOs and LAs – proposed to be mandatory in future for FCs. Palliative care also at home.	Home care and home nursing 2 x per week. 80% HH from LAs, 13% from NGOs, private – 10%	Some services free e.g. rehab, HH for terminally ill, nursing care at home, lab tests at home. Client fees e.g. doctor – 22 € p.a. max. PHC emergency – max 15 € for home nursing- depending on household income and size- fee varies from 11-35 € Tax reductions available for purchase of domestic work. Some contribution for costs of day care. (some free thru' LA, some private / NGO and paid for) Respite partly paid for by FC.	**Good quality control** – Govt. provides national recommendations- and citizens asked regularly for comments by LAs. **Training**- Good all trained. Only qualified can get a job. Have project to promote work ability and maintain well being at work because of high turn over.
France	**Home Help** and **Local coordination centres** –Access to a home-helper and other domiciliary services (nursing excluded) is not a legal right. **Day Care centres** – some, more needed **Home health care** - comprehensive including hospitalization at home, paramedical service. delivery of drugs, Access is a legal right. **Dementia services** – some; more	Regions vary - Multitude of private and public organizations based on different financial sources. Regional variations in range of services: other services include accompanying, adaptation of the home, administrative help, home alarm, keeping company, meals, mobile library, repairs, shopping, technical help,	Means tested for children of OP. Nursing and other paramedical community services are financed by the N.H.I; higher income recipients can be asked for co-financing. H.H is financed from numerous private and public sources Other services e.g. house alarm systems or meals on	**Adequate quality control** Regional authority responsible for management / supervision provided in the APA programme. Special computer programs developed for quality control (& in residential care). NGOs elaborate with staff, individual quality plans based on their definitions, aims, and expectations. **Training**. Inadequate – many

Countries	Availability of Home Based services Home Help and Local coordination centres; Day Care centres; Public sector; Home Health care – Dementia services; Respite care in the home	Additional comments	Costs of using service care Affordability	Quality & control of service – ISO. Training of Workers
	needed Respite care – yes and also includes granny sitting and day or night care at home.	transportation, tutelage	wheels often financed by the regional government with co-funding from recipient.	untrained Low impact of new care diploma as unskilled HH staff easily find work & certification has no impact on salary.
Germany	Home Help and Local coordination centres 1 in 15 aged 75 + get home care. 18% of households. Day Care centres – Growth; available if FC cannot be guaranteed or if day care is necessary to ease the burden on family carers. Home health care - comprehensive Dementia services - some, inadequate and need expanding Respite care - some	HH by NGOs and profit companies and offer nursing care + different kinds of HH. (N = 3,622) said OP in need of care or help doesn't receive enough. Complementary services e.g. shopping, visiting, accompanying to doctors and other local services, gardening and household maintenance not offered despite high need for such "light" services. Regional variations e.g. Bremen SC services include: Meals on wheels, FC counselling / discussion groups, organizing domestic care giving, help with authorities, filling forms, household tasks, laundry, cooking, walks, visiting the doctor and collecting prescribed remedies	Means tested social assistance is available to finance HH. The OP or FC contract with the social service centre where amount and type of assistance is laid down. The contract costs 20,- € p.m. and every service hour after that costs 7,15 €. This sum is seen as compensation for the mostly voluntary workers. If HH is needed and no need for care determined then the OP or the FC must pay for it. Community care and meals on wheels are refinanced either by the personal contributions from the consumer or partly from the social welfare office. Day care - When OP are entitled to benefits the LTCI pays all care-related costs over an indefinite period. Social care is paid for as well as medical treatment care	Inadequate quality control 2001 additional legislation to guarantee certain quality levels through the LTCI. LTCI and service providers must agree contracts, regulating quality standards but these refer only to structures and process rather than outcomes of care No general monitoring body which lays down criteria for the assessment of service quality in out-patient health care. Training – adequate –mostly trained The family carer / social assistant are qualified No state controlled training programme but specialist community care training is offered by various educational institutions.

Countries	Availability of Home Based services Home Help and Local coordination centres; Day Care centres; Public sector; Home Health care – Dementia services; Respite care in the home	Additional comments	Costs of using service care Affordability	Quality & control of service – ISO. Training of Workers

Countries	Availability of Home Based services Home Help and Local coordination centres; Day Care centres; Public sector; Home Health care – Dementia services; Respite care in the home	Additional comments	Costs of using service care Affordability	Quality & control of service – ISO. Training of Workers
Greece	**Home Help and Local coordination centres** A third (253) of LAs have home help services in 285 operating units; 47% of users lived alone. Growth in coverage. Some coordinated with social & health centres for OP. **Day Care centres** – a few have just started **Home health care** - Inadequate **Dementia services** – a few support services **Respite care** – no services	.	Free at point of use. Although primarily designed for OP alone, many cover FCs that need support. Private care – limited home services except for resident migrant workers – costing approx 5-600 € wages + low rate of insurance for those who are legitimate. Cheaper than residential care. Health care requires informal payments especially for home visits.	**Inadequate quality control** Administrative criteria. **Training – Adequate. Mostly trained** Home help services – headed by trained SW.
Hungary	**Home Help and Local coordination centres** 2% of 60+ receive HH. 4.5% of OP get institutional help from the LA in case of illness and nursing; proportion highest in Budapest (8.2%) and lowest in villages (3.3%). **Day Care centres** – some have started **Home health care** - Inadequate **Dementia services** – **Respite care** – some in day care centres have started	Run by LAs as mandatory service. LA may contract out the task to a civil organisation or market actor under an agreement or contract. 22.9% of all recipients of HH lived in small ageing settlements 12.6% of all persons receiving meals. Hot meals important. family help centres support FCS of all kinds	Free for FCs. Funding through LAs and numerous NGOs – 70,000– 15% for health / social care. Funded by state (26.2%), own revenues (52.7%) and private support Hungarian Red Cross and the Hungarian Maltese Charity Service play important role in providing a high standard service free of charge and innovatory. All FCs and OP in need are eligible. Health care requires informal payments	**Adequate quality control** Budapest Public Administration Office using experts of 2 nonstate institutions (Foundation for Social Innovation, Hungarian Association of Social Directors) – HH also supervised by Methodology Centre of the Hungarian Maltese Charity service. But inadequate integration between health and social services. **Training – Adequate. Mostly trained** carers in the home help service are nurses Participation in training on quality assurance

Countries	Availability of Home Based services Home Help and Local coordination centres; Day Care centres; Public sector; Home Health care – Dementia services; Respite care in the home	Additional comments	Costs of using service care Affordability	Quality & control of service – ISO. Training of Workers
		.		is important

Countries	Availability of Home Based services Home Help and Local coordination centres; Day Care centres; Public sector; Home Health care – Dementia services; Respite care in the home	Additional comments	Costs of using service care Affordability	Quality & control of service – ISO. Training of Workers
Ireland	**Home Help and Local coordination centres** 80% recipients elderly, less than 1 / 30 get service Provision by health boards. 5% aged 75+. 2007 aim is to cover 25% of those aged 75+ (by 2020 estimated 5% of 80+.pop. and 10% 60+ in need of care) 133,000 of which 15,901 (2% government supported) Limited private home care **Day Care centres** –. Inadequate coverage e.g. home care, day centres. Large expansion planned **Home health care** Good GP, Therapy 3% **Dementia services** – some thru' NGOs, more planned in HN services and day care centres **Respite care**- partial - regional variations by the health board or NGOs	Inadequate HH and Day Care in coverage and amount, and geographical inequalities. a, type of condition / disability etc. Unclear entitlement, anomalies and inequalities Chiropody very popular – 16% (of a sample of 937 in HeSSOP study) use it 12% would have liked to use it but could not access the service. All health boards provide HH but depends on demand. Barrier to use – lack of knowledge 14% find it difficult. Stigma- 30% for meals on wheels & 20% Home Help	medical card (for low income individuals and families and free for all aged 70+) Private services depend on income. Tax relief for employment of private carer– means-testing Applies to all services	**Inadequate quality control** No usually in place. Line management – discrete reporting system. **Training**- Inadequate. Many untrained The above applies to home help only Workers in day care centres, dementia and respite services all undergo training.
Italy	**Home Help and Local coordination centres** 1% of 65+ get home care services discrimination against rural areas and southern regions. Inadequate coverage and demand exceeds provision. **Day Care centres** integrated centres are very positive **Home health care** - partial, regional differences	Problematic relationship between families and the public service network, where services considered the most helpful are, at the same time, perceived as the most inadequate (community care centres, availability of medicines, home care	Monetary transfers in south and rural areas are often the only kind of support available to family carers because of the lack of services.	**Inadequate quality control** LAs control and accredit but no clear norms and definitions. They fund and identify minimum service standards to accredit all those providers that respond to these requirements. **Training**- partial - yes for professional level. But for lower

Countries	Availability of Home Based services Home Help and Local coordination centres; Day Care centres; Public sector; Home Health care – Dementia services; Respite care in the home	Additional comments	Costs of using service care Affordability	Quality & control of service – ISO. Training of Workers
	Dementia services - partial **Respite care** – none at home	assistance, specialized health centres for Alzheimer's disease, monetary provisions and home health care)		level workers attempts at Regional level, but many unqualified.
Luxembourg	**Home Help** and **Local coordination centres.** Yes. Min. 3.5 hrs per week to qualify for OP (dependent person) No private services **Day Care centres** – yes 7 centres run by an NGO for psycho-geriatric cases **Home health care** - comprehensive **Dementia services** -yes **Respite care** – yes (3 wks per year) and financed by dependency insurance.	2 Foundations in charge of aids and services within framework of dependency insurance. One of their coordinators visits OP and FC after notification from Union of Sickness Funds. NGOs running respite care services funded by Ministry.	All needing help covered by dependency insurance. Partially qualified under SI become eligible after 1 year. Dependent OP receives nursing allowance of 23.85 € p.h. that can be used to benefit FC. > 7 hours care p.w. can be used by informal carer. 7-14 hrs – service networks must provide half the hours. 14+ hours per week – completely provided by help services. Dependent OP receives annually double the amount of nursing allowance to finance respite care and give FC time for recreation. Temporary stay in nursing homes directly financed by dependency insurance	**Adequate quality control** Public evaluation center (CEO) provides estimates of needs for care and of benefits needed under the dependency insurance. CEO advises the Union of Sickness Funds who classify dependency, pay for nursing services, negotiate with services for provision of nursing aids. Further quality development assurance under development. **Training.**- Adequate Mostly trained, plans to extend training
Malta	**Home Help** and **Local coordination centres** Yes. 30 different services to maintaining OP in community. Services include Handyman Service, Home Care Help, Incontinence Service, Meals on	Cases discussed by Internal Board of Allocation of Service after application and medical report; on acceptance goes to	Free Some private agencies provide home and nursing care;	**Adequate quality control** Internal Board of Allocation of Service **Training**- Good- Mostly trained

Countries	Availability of Home Based services	Additional comments	Costs of using service care Affordability	Quality & control of service – ISO. Training of Workers
	Home Help and Local coordination centres; Day Care centres; Public sector; Home Health care – Dementia services; Respite care in the home			
	Wheels, Telecare, etc. Waiting lists Day Care centres –5% of OP in 14 areas Home health care - Comprehensive including Domiciliary Nursing Dementia services – in day hospital, plus advice thru NGO. Respite care – some organised by NGO.	the area supervisor where OP lives; allocation of hours of service to OP made on basis of real needs. Many FCs using HH services feel it an admission of their inability to live up to family expectations, leading to an uneasy partnership between FCs and formal service providers.	charges depend on the number of hours service used. But not easily affordable by every family.	2 weeks training prior to recruitment. For part time Social Assistants 446, mainly employed as Home helps with very small no. of OP as clients with PTSAs selected from the same area of the beneficiaries in her care. Others e.g. Memorial District Nursing Association, professionally trained.
Netherlands	Home Help and Local coordination centres regional integrated needs assessment agencies; only 1 in 5 chronically ill or disabled persons uses professional assistance. Day Care centres 17% uses care attendance facilities and 10% reports that the person they care for visit day care facilities or activity centres Home health care - Comprehensive Dementia services – yes, some pilot projects* Respite care – yes a wide range of forms at home, day care, by formal services and NGOs	36% of FCs do not arrange formal home care because the care receivers do not want strangers in their house FCs of someone receiving formal home care also more often use support services for FCs (information, advice and emotional support services) (48% V29% of the care receivers without formal home care). Professional HH restricted to few tasks: washing / bathing, dressing OP, heavy household	Needs assessment. Personal care budget so people buy own care and many small private home care organisations are arising. Yes out of pocket payments – 53% reported no difficulties in meeting these. OP after assessment and if eligible for non-institutional care, can ask for care in cash or kind. And can use it to pay FC / kin	**Adequate quality control.** Independent organisation monitor the large home care organisations which can receive a quality sign. Organisations work with care plans (set up together with patient); Privacy guarantee; Client / residents' committees; Independent Complaints committees. Small private home care organisations not monitored and controlled by government **Training.** Adequate Mostly trained compulsory for all levels except the lowest level

Countries	Availability of Home Based services: Home Help and Local coordination centres; Day Care centres; Public sector; Home Health care – Dementia services; Respite care in the home	Additional comments	Costs of using service care / Affordability	Quality & control of service – ISO. / Training of Workers
		tasks if there is no FC or when there's a longstanding and intensive care situation and transfer to intramural care is threatened.		
Norway	**Home Help and Local coordination centres** LA provided. 30% elderly 75+ received formal home help services. 30% of the non-institutional population 67+ in need of help to shop and clean. 5% needed care from others or could hardly manage to dress or take care of their daily personal hygiene on their own. **Day Care centres** – yes in nearly all LA areas except very small LAs. **Home health care** - comprehensive including locally available statutory rehabilitation facilities **Dementia services** – 80% of LAs have special dementia services, and increasing no. to support FCs. **Respite care**- yes by LAs and NGOs	LA responsibility; family provides less instrumental and personal care, but total level of help (from family and services) in Norway is higher than in countries with more family dominated care systems But insufficient public services, and families supply more care than they find reasonable. Some FCs give care at the cost of their own health and welfare.	Part co-payment. LA pays All in need- disability based, Individual entitlement – even if FC available.	**Adequate quality control.** Supervision legislation. LA responsible. **Training**- Good, Most trained
Poland	**Home Help and Local coordination centres** Social care at LA, county, region. In 2002 LA services were used by 81.2 thousand people 2-3 times per week, 2 hours services	Community assistance includes financial assistance (mainly permanent, temporary and intentional benefits) and services – (e.g. home nursing ser-	HH dependent on the income and estimated needs of all the members of the household Free. But co-payments for	**Inadequate quality control.** Administrative mainly. NGOs - control is restricted to the financial aspects and legal basis of their activity and fulfil-

Countries	Availability of Home Based services Home Help and Local coordination centres; Day Care centres; Public sector; Home Health care – Dementia services; Respite care in the home	Additional comments	Costs of using service care Affordability	Quality & control of service – ISO. Training of Workers
	Day Care centres - LAs; Nos decreasing.- 213 **Dementia services** – not at home **Home health care** - inadequate **Respite care**- no	vices, laundry services). no social services market, which would allow social care centres to buy services for elderly and disabled from NGOS or private Cos. 418.300 (160.700 1 person households.) households. ¾ in cities. N.B. Earlier attempts to integrate H and SS led to lower status of soc. Care workers – current separation has increased equality	medicines are heavy burden for FCs,. Plus payments to attend private clinics	ing their contracts. **Training.** Adequate 6,500 employees in Social Care Centres + many volunteers and employees in NGOs + 11,000 Social Care Centres employing 11,000 for specialised care.
Portugal	Home Help and **Local coordination** centres – attempts to integrate H and SS. **Day Care** centres growth in nos. 41,195 places in 1998 **Home health care** - inadequate **Dementia services** - no **Respite care**- not in home, rare		Small charge for day care Costs for using some health services at home.	**Inadequate quality control.** SW specialists undertake control and consultations. Control of economy of social care institutions based on annual (or quarterly) activity reports. Control over NGOs limited to their service contracts and the financial support from the ministry. Most of this control is restricted to financial aspects and legal basis of the NGO's activity. **Training** – inadequate- some attempts to start wider training.
Slovenia	**Home Help** and **Local coordination** centres around 5,000 people receive	The current organisational crisis in health care	LA vary but social home assistance subsidised approx.	**Inadequate quality control.**

Countries	Availability of Home Based services Home Help and Local coordination centres; Day Care centres; Public sector; Home Health care – Dementia services; Respite care in the home	Additional comments	Costs of using service care Affordability	Quality & control of service – ISO. Training of Workers
	public home help. by 52 centres for social work, 5 old people's homes and 3 private providers **Day Care centres** 20 OP homes had centres; with capacity for around 300 people **Home health care** - inadequate **Dementia services** – NGOs have started support services **Respite care** – no	system has substantially reduced nursing care. Physical condition	70%. This service is not equally developed in all municipalities. Numbers of social carers declining because of lack of funding for LAs.	**Training** – mixed - inadequate. qualified home help staff= 660; Home assistants can be experts or persons who obtained 1 yr training for home social carers, confirmed by the Social Chamber of Slovenia. (1 year part time- 168 school hours. The position of a social carer is not a health profession. Trained *nurse-carers*
Spain	**Home Help and Local coordination centres** Sharp Increase in demand. (75% in 3 yrs) 2.80% of 65+ attended by HH service. 1 in 15 of those aged 75+. mainly women (over 60%); 53% < 80 yrs. Av. 3.5-4 hours a week per person, mean cost 9.5 €. p.h. 1.48% 65+ get public tele-assistance service, in 10+ of the 17 autonomous communities, increase in demand by 114.75%. 70% + of HH undertaken in private sector. Only 8% of population would wish to be attended only by the public SS and 12% would wish to be attended by the family and the SS together. **Day Care centres** 0.11% dependent	HH care programmes in Catalonia in 90% of the primary care centres, more than 75% offer carer training and almost 69% specific "caring for the carer' programmes.	Co-payments. Home help is expensive- the hourly service costs more than 17 €). Where OP received the funding (or the FC) they use money for irregular contracts by the hour, without assuming the corresponding labour costs, so the municipal money contributes to nurturing the submerged economy daily In a day centre, they must contribute 25% of their pension	**Inadequate quality control.** LAs responsible but doubtful quality poor mechanisms of coordination between services; general scarcity of the service and the high levels of co-payment. **Training** – inadequate for Professionals- their profile not always suitable for the work, especially in supervision and management; the scarce interest of the workers in jobs concerning the hygiene and personal attention to the OP; the general poor connection between the workers and the users;

Countries	Availability of Home Based services Home Help and Local coordination centres; Day Care centres; Public sector; Home Health care – Dementia services; Respite care in the home	Additional comments	Costs of using service care Affordability	Quality & control of service – ISO. Training of Workers
	people used a service, **Home health care** - inadequate **Dementia services** - no **Respite care** - no			
Sweden	**Home Help** and **Local coordination centres** LA decide service level, eligibility criteria and range of services. Single-entry system; OP helped by LA where he lives. 2003, 8% 65 years + got HH. Of 80+, 19% got HH i.e. despite growth in population numbers HH less but contact hours increased successively i.e. fewer persons get more help. 28% get HH in the evenings and night. Comprehensive LA services e.g. transportation services, foot care, meals on wheels, security alarms, housing adaptations, handicap aids, etc. LAs started FC resource centres offering training, counselling, support groups, respite care, and other information and resources for family caregivers **Day Care centres** - **Yes** programs for disabled family member **Home health care** - comprehensive. 2.7% 65+ get home nursing care **Dementia services** - Yes	Need assessment by LA care manager. In some LAs interdisciplinary care planning teams for assessment and co-ordination of eldercare services frequent, especially concerning a permanent move to institutional care. 4% of all OP with HH received more than 120 hours p.m..	Co-payment but there is a cap on how much the user pays, to ensure they have income left for their own expenses. In more than half of all municipalities, care management is based on a purchaser – provider model. Private, out of pocket paid health care is extremely unusual	**Adequate quality control.** LA monitors plus supervision by the National Board of Health and Welfare (focusing health care issues and based on the Health Care Act) and the county Administrative Board (focusing social service issues and based on the Social Services Act). **Training.** Good 192 000 persons (home helpers / nurses aids) were employed in the home help services. 25% were full-time employed, nearly 60 per cent worked part-time and the rest were on an hourly basis employment.

Countries	Availability of Home Based services Home Help and Local coordination centres; Day Care centres; Public sector; Home Health care – Dementia services; Respite care in the home	Additional comments	Costs of using service care Affordability	Quality & control of service – ISO. Training of Workers
	Respite care- yes			
Switzerland	**Home Help and Local coordination centres** – large variations between cantons; some provide HH others do not.	Cannot generalize results as cantons implement very different policies in H & SS	Costs of home nursing not fully covered by HI	**Adequate quality control. Training-** only for health personnel. Inadequate for others.
	Day Care centres – some, unequal coverage, attached to hospitals or run by NGOs e.g. Spitex	a third of the elderly declare they don't want home care services because they don't want foreigners at home.	The economic value of FC work has been calculated to reach between 10 and 12 billions of Swiss Francs, exceeding the cumulated spending of both the HC services and the OP home of Switzerland	
	Home health care - comprehensive. Palliative care at home also available			
	Dementia services – 90,000 persons affected by Alzheimer			
	Respite care- very little.			
UK	**Home Help and Local coordination centres.** LAs now give more intensive services to less users. 2002 av. contact hours for each of the supported 366,800 households = 8.1 hours. 41% of those needing care get visits from H&SS or volunteers	Whether the household was involved in heavy care did not add significantly to the likelihood of using services.	After assessment by Social services- means and needs tested.	**Adequate quality control.** Social services - line management and reporting systems back through to an Executive Director.
	64% provided by the independent sectors, up from 42% 5 years ago	(41%) of cared-for people (of all age groups) receive visits from health, social or voluntary services. Visits lower if lived		External providers such as voluntary organisations or commercial sectors are managed by their own managers / owners / committee / board. National Care Standards Commission guarantees quality.
	Day Care centres 65-74 year age group, 32% of cared-for people attend some form of daily club or day care / hospital, with the figure being 29% in those aged 85 and over	with FC carer (23%) V in another household (50) e.g. home help / meals on wheels (9% / 31%).		All purchased home care services are delivered under contract with a legal Form of
	Home health care - comprehensive	People living in the same		

Countries	Availability of Home Based services	Additional comments	Costs of using service care Affordability	Quality & control of service – ISO. Training of Workers
	Home Help and Local coordination centres; Day Care centres; Public sector; Home Health care – Dementia services; Respite care in the home with chiropody and HV or district nurse being most popular. **Dementia services** – Alzheimer Assoc. has 25,000 members,300 branches and support groups; gives information and education for people with dementia, FCs. & professionals. runs quality day and home care, **Respite care**- yes, was the essential service in supporting FCs but funding no longer guaranteed for this purpose.	household as the carer are less likely to receive visits from health practitioners (15% / 30%		Agreement and a detailed Service Specification. Theses are subject to quarterly monitoring, Annual Services Reviews and independent service user surveys run by SSD Contracts Unit. ISOs. **Training** – adequate

5.9 Annex 9 – Matrix: Care of dependent older People – current and future Supply of formal and informal Care Givers

Country	Family carers	Trends in availability of FC — Combining work and care	Public services, labour supply and trends	Private services	Volunteers	Migrant carers	Training: 1. family carers 2. formal carers 3. volunteers
Austria	40% work and care. above av. For those with low status jobs. 55% lived with or adjacent to OP. 2 / 3 of dependent OP get FC. Only 0.5% of Austrians list no one upon whom they can rely in minor cases of need. In serious cases of need as well there are few people (1.7%) who consider themselves without any support from relatives or friends.	Better educated + those with better jobs less willing to care.	Low wage sector- 7.5-8 pr hour. Problems I getting help at weekends and night. Shortage of home health nurses.	Yes- re-privatization of care.	Yes. Young men can undertake care instead of military service	Large grey LM of migrants as care and domestic workers from E Europe. E.g. Czech Republic or Hungary. Estimated costs for a 24-hour in-home service are around 1,400 € p.m..	1. Yes – partly paid for- done by NGOs and LA 2. Yes – no national regulations or standards 3. Yes- some but many not trained
Belgium	5.89% of Belgians 16+ were caring without pay for someone who is ill, dependent or elderly.2 / 3 cared for by family – no change Maj aged 44-76, 69.33% female. 66.36% married. More likely than non carers to be pensioners, housewives or unemployed. Of those in paid work, 30% in	Greater mobility and less FC available makes future care difficult. Belgian LM-53.37% men, 31.92% women aged 50-65 active in LM	Demand for home services larger than supply Difficulties in finding certifies nurses Good residential care. Govt. attempting	No informal unregistered carers. Na data	Yes – sit in	No data	1. Yes – from subsidized carers' groups 2. Yes 3. Yes- sit in services.

Country	Family carers	Trends in availability of FC — Combining work and care	Public services, labour supply and trends	Private services	Volunteers	Migrant carers	Training 1. family carers 2. formal carers 3. volunteers
	pt / time. 39.26% 15 hrs per week; 4% stopped temp. work because of caring. Av 17.5 hrs care per week (1 > 99) 59% live in same household. 14.89% husbands, 46.82 parents, 14.33% in laws, other family cared for 16.99% non family = 13.31% Breakdown by those needing care and age.	2 / 3 of care from families but OP think families less willing to care.	to improve working conditions and wages. 11,000 self employed nurses – 30% not ft / time in self empl. but work in hospitals				
Bulgaria	20% unemployment and 1 million émigrés leaves many OP without FCs	Unknown	Inadequate, bad, irregular pay. But a large supply of qualified personnel.	Yes- growth in hire of private carers (through migrant remittances)	Yes.	-	1. – 2. Yes 3. Yes for volunteers
Czech Republic	Children (53%), spouse (21%), friends (16%) and relatives (10%). FCs- 64% women 36% of men. 80% of care provided at home. Approx. 100 000 seniors need assistance with basic ADL, about 300 000 seniors need assistance with IADL- approx. 400- 500 000 FCs. The average time period of this type of care is 4-5 years. Women of LM age are the	High rates of employment amongst women till 55.	Even in regions with a high unemployment rate there may be vacancies in social care. The level of income received by caring professionals is so low that many people prefer to stay rather unem-			No data but some from ex Soviet Union in non registered domestic work	–

Country	Family carers	Trends in availability of FC — Combining work and care	Public services, labour supply and trends	Private services	Volunteers	Migrant carers	Training — 1. family carers 2. formal carers 3. volunteers
	most frequent caregivers. 80% are employed.		ployed than to work with older people.				
Denmark	Max. 55% OP get help with certain tasks with primary providers being spouses and children – but no accurate data – Most help is for house, transport.	female labour force participation rates one of highest Aged 44-50 expect to spend more time with FC than older generations.	100,000 full-time employees. 2.001 to 2002, the% growth in the number of full-time employees in the care sector for older people at 4.4 per cent was more than three times the growth in the number of older people aged 80 years and over in that year (1.4 per cent). Training aims to address recruitment problems in the care (for older people) sector. 90% female- attempts to attract men.	Same as public	Yes	No data – limited use of private works but 120,000 foreign workers of whom 20 per cent were from central and Eastern European countries and 24 per cent were from Asia	1. – 2. Yes- basic training system in phases, increase motivation for further training 14-20 months for domestic work, and over 95% of those working with older people have this level of training. Trainees receive a salary as a trained working care worker. 3. –

Country	Family carers	Trends in availability of FC / Combining work and care	Public services, labour supply and trends	Private services	Volunteers	Migrant carers	Training 1. family carers 2. formal carers 3. volunteers
Finland	43% spouses, 22% children, 22% parents (all kinds of FCs) 30% aged 18-49 33% 40-64 39% 65+ Men 25% of FCs More single person households of 75 + years	Huge increase in no of Older women working and attempts to increase this further Shortages foreseen Increase in no. of men carers Shortage of working age people.	Problem of retention low salaries and emigrate to work elsewhere.	Increase of 25% in personnel	Yes esp. pensioners. But NGOs need volunteers. Informal care accounts for only 1% of care.	Low availability	1. yes by Carers associations 2. yes 3. Finnish Red Cross and Church
France	Nos increased with decline of older women's LM participation. 3,2% in residential homes, 0,6% profess help only. Low LM participation of group 55 to 64 years	Developing mainly thru NGOs	Shortage of nurses in hospitals. No shortage in the other sectors (except of qualified home-helpers, but many services easily recruit unskilled home-helpers).	Few	Large civil orgs – NGOs providing many volunteers. Neighbours very important	Yes but no data	1. Yes 2. Yes but often not taken up 3. Yes for volunteers
Germany	60% 55+ Unemployed / unskilled. Civil servants, self employed	More educated in ft employment. Decline in norms on FC.	Service led, not needs led. Shortages, a lot of overtime.	Yes – much non declared. Large variety to meet needs of house-	Yes. Volunteers compensated.	Est. 50,000 migrants as care workers. Many paid thru LTCI	1. some - free 2. Yes- in all areas

Country	Family carers	Trends in availability of FC Combining work and care	Public services, labour supply and trends	Private services	Volunteers	Migrant carers	Training 1. family carers 2. formal carers 3. volunteers
	and salaried combine work with FC, M / c accept residential care. FCs caring for OP not suffering from dementia significantly more engaged in LM (30,9%) than those taking care of OP suffering from dementia (25,3%).	LTCI helped women retreat from FC. P25 – differences in attitudes to FC by age groups.	(despite high unemployment rates) Dramatic problems, inadequate provision, 20,000 new jobs would have to be created in LTC to fill all existing and new jobs and to reduce the amount of overtime. 27,000 unemployed. geriatric care professionals at Federal Labour Office; quality of applicants qualifications also deteriorating	holds. 1994 4 mill. Households employed domestic help		but many still illegal. Private households 2nd largest employer in grey LM. Work permits now permitted, unknown take up and avoidance because of higher costs for soc. Insurance.	3. Yes
Greece	Estimated 636,114 aged 60+ need part or full time care. No data on numbers of FCs. Men increasingly involved as FCs 29% of all households care for someone who is depend-	Attempts to increase LF participation of women- but currently low especially for older women	Low prestige of job and generally low pay make many decide that it is not a desirable labour choice.	Some signs of private services of nurses starting for the better off.	Orthodox Church and other churches run voluntary services that include FC	Yes- many workers, 13% estimated in domestic work and many of these in care for OP- rough estimate	1. some 2. some 3. some

Country	Family carers	Trends in availability of FC\nCombining work and care	Public services, labour supply and trends	Private services	Volunteers	Migrant carers	Training\n1. family carers\n2. formal carers\n3. volunteers
	ent; this includes children, the dependent disabled as well as dependent older people.	Overall traditional low numbers entering nursing.			support. Orthodox had 23,000 giving several hours of voluntary work per year. But low levels overall of voluntarism.	that 6.4% of Greek households employed someone to help OP.	
Hungary	Of all OP. 11.3% relied on daughters and 8.7% sons. Brothers declined to 1.5%, slight increase in help by sisters 4.1% Increase in nos of sons as carers because of late marriage.\n\nRural areas adoption of young people (19.2% OP rely on friends) and (34.4%) neighbours as FCs. Spouse, Ds and sons most import FCs.	Low / declining LM activity rate for women – huge increase in availability. Live less with OP.\n\nVery little pt / time work\n\nNo changes in amount of Fc given to OP. But numbers of potential FCs steadily declines for OP.	Inadequate nursing.\n\nShortages of workers in public sector, low wages, low status. Mainly women.	Hardly any because of economic situation of OP.	Available and as employees, at lower wages than public sector. Important in providing services to OP.\n\nMen as alternative to military service\n\nHuge increase in civil organizations- 70,000 NGOs, 13% in health and care fields.	No	1. –\n2. Most have training.\nSome innovative training from NGOs for young people to become carers. 90% of employees of NGOs are trained compared to 60–70% for the public sector.\n3. yes- some - important
Ireland	Huge increase in LM partici-	Demographic	4.6% in nursing	Large private	The voluntary	No statistical	1. Yes – 13 week

Country	Family carers	Trends in availability of FC Combining work and care	Public services, labour supply and trends	Private services	Volunteers	Migrant carers	Training 1. family carers 2. formal carers 3. volunteers
	pation of women to 50% (2003) and highest rate of increase for those aged 45-64 yrs. 1 / 3 worked part time. 38.6% male, 61.4% female (Census 2002) Half FC provide care for parents / in-law; 1 in 4 for spouse; 1in 5 another relative. 5-6% of adults as carers- 154,000-185,000 of which 133,000 and 159,000 adults of working age In Carers Clinics 43% were 60+ 22% 7=80 25% men	bulge of people aged 65+ will be in 2040s. Women carers have marginally lower rates of employment (47.4%) as women not caring (50.9%). Increase in no. of men carers. Women may be less willing to care in future with formal employment rising, and greater demand for support from govt., public service. Still majority of women FCs not in paid employment No relation between higher education and hours of caring.	home care. Growing demand Services generally under-funded and under-staffed especially: nursing therapies chiropody respite community / home-based services home help Poor pay and working conditions for home helps and no promotion. HH not attractive to work with older people. Some staff shortages	sector – hospital, nursing home, therapies, home nursing among others. 48% of the population avail of care as private patients in public hospitals or in private hospitals. Some staff shortages in private sector especially nursing	sector is a significant provider of services in community, primary, hospital, long-stay and respite care. The HSE funds voluntary organisations to provide services it cannot provide itself. Voluntary organisations are sometimes provided through the religious organisations, but many are independent and community-based.	data available, anecdotal evidence of some migrant women working in domestic and care sectors	modular skills training in 17 locations 2. Training provided by voluntary organisations for home care personnel. While recommendations made regarding certification of home helps, these recommendations have not yet been implemented by Government. 3. –

Country	Family carers	Trends in availability of FC Combining work and care	Public services, labour supply and trends	Private services	Volunteers	Migrant carers	Training 1. family carers 2. formal carers 3. volunteers
Italy	75-80% of elderly care is carried out in the informal network of an extended family. Increase in FC age (61 men, 60 women), in nos of sons caring but 2 / 3 women are the FCs rising to 81% for heavy care. 10% are over 80 years Decline in multi-generation households. Carers have more income than non carers. 60% not happy with economic situation. Working women give less time to care. Carers have a higher education level than non carers	Decline because of increase in numbers of women in LM (20% in 1970 to 36% IN 2003) and increase in retirement age.	Local labour supply of home care workers for OP much lower than the demand, since local people unwilling to accept a job that is considered tiring and wearing. Trend of State in providing more cash not services. (used by carers to purchase in private services) 756,446 care allowances were granted to Italian citizens of over 65 years of age, for a total cost of 3,622,322,940 €	600-700,000, 50% of total registered workers are foreigners. Used for home and night care, used in private hospitals. And public for night care "badanti" (privately paid carers	A number of self help and advocacy groups and active in some areas. (www.aimaroma.it)	Attitude of local workforce has increased recourse to foreign workers who, at least during the first period of their stay in Italy, more ready to work in occupational sectors that are characterized by great uncertainty and are considered menial by the locals Thus a large and growing number, many illegal. Increasing efforts to legalise them.	1. – 2. Yes for those employed in formal institutions and services. But few migrants – 94% have training (though often educated highly, 36% of families' personal assistants (36%) and 16% of employed home care workers have none or a just sufficient understanding of the Italian language 3.
Luxembourg	465 FCs recorded as giving help to family member- 94.2% female. – mean age 43.7 - Mostly serving people aged 70+ (80%)		Overall no current shortages since wages are high and attract workers from	Some beginning to emerge		More than half in health and social services are of foreign origin (mainly other EU	–

Country	Family carers	Trends in availability of FC / Combining work and care	Public services, labour supply and trends	Private services	Volunteers	Migrant carers	Training / 1. family carers / 2. formal carers / 3. volunteers
			neighbouring countries; but long term fear of shortages in nursing personnel evidenced by decline in enrolment in Nursing School.			countries)	
Malta	Of the 259 family carers benefiting from the Government's Carer's Pension 59% cent were females as compared to 41% men. Another study had 74% of FCs female. 74.5% of interviewed FCs were child FCs. 78.7% respondents in one research cohabitant with OP. 18.1 per cent lived between 1-2 kilometres away. Low (31%) LM participation of women 16-64. Some evidence of increasing male participation in FC	Decline because of increases in numbers of OP, residential mobility and increasing LM participation of women. But more OP involved in care of grandchildren	Decline in numbers entering religious vocations (nuns) has led to increasing reliance on paid lay workers. However no difficulties in recruitment for part time care workers.	However no difficulties in recruitment for part time care workers.	A lot of work thru Church with elderly Good Neighbour Scheme; Social Clubs; Self-Health Care; Awareness Programmes in Schools	No	1. Yes 2. Yes- available but not compulsory in private sector. 3. The volunteers of each group, 85 per cent of whom are themselves elderly, receive training given by Caritas social workers at the headquarters. They also attend refresher seminars organised every 3 months.

Country	Family carers	Trends in availability of FC Combining work and care	Public services, labour supply and trends	Private services	Volunteers	Migrant carers	Training 1. family carers 2. formal carers 3. volunteers
Nether-lands	no nation-wide registration of FCs. 3,7 million – 29% of Dutch population over 18 years – provided care for a relative, friend or neighbour in need in 2001. More than two million people took care of someone 64 + years. 400,000 (18.8%) intense and long term. Age breakdown of Fc show more aged 54% = aged 45-64 The preference for help from relatives / acquaintances has declined especially among higher educated people. They more often call for assistance from private care-givers	71% of FCs aged18-65 years, of whom 60% active at the LM-set to increase. Some care leave. Being developed work leaves:. FCs same rates of employment as the general population (64% of the people between 18 and 65 years), and same education level. FCs, who work fulltime provide less hours per week than FCs with a part-time job or without a job. Increase of female L.M. participation, migration away from			Yes- volunteers also funded by govt.	Low - 4.15 –6% of the migrant population in nursing and caring jobs. The greatest impediment for entering this part of the LM is requirement for higher education and poor command of the Dutch language.	1. yes 2 Yes – but not for lower levels tho' opportunities for on the job training exist.

Country	Family carers	Trends in availability of FC / Combining work and care	Public services, labour supply and trends	Private services	Volunteers	Migrant carers	Training 1. family carers 2. formal carers 3. volunteers
		parents) and ageing of FCs affect trends in FC. growing tendency that more people may choose not to care.					
Norway	5% respondents 16-74 gave some care / help to adults in own household in 2000 (due to old age, disability or illness). = 160,000 people. 8% - or approximately 255,000 people - helped people in other households. Care / help given by people aged 75+ not included. Total informal care received by people aged 67+ from people in own as well as other households, amounted to 49,000 man years. Women give 2.5 times as much family care as men. The gender difference is at its smallest for the oldest caregivers	The proportion of the population aged 16-74 giving family care as well as time spent on family care has been somewhat reduced from 1990 to 2000 people in low income households give help to other households. But overall FC has not been reduced, but has rather in-	Shortages esp. in urban areas- high turnover	Some are developing	Yes- both informal (neighbours and friends) and formal in NGOs.	Legal migrants important unskilled care workers. Also legally and illegally in private homes. Mainly housework and to a very small extent care work for the elderly.	1. Some 2. yes- but not all employees trained 3. yes

Country	Family carers	Trends in availability of FC — Combining work and care	Public services, labour supply and trends	Private services	Volunteers	Migrant carers	Training — 1. family carers 2. formal carers 3. volunteers
		creased, in the last 30 years					
Poland	FC- daughter 37.1%), spouse (29.2%), son (20.9%), grandchildren (15.5%), 92% of OP believe that in case of sickness they can count on help from their families	No special leave. About 1.3 work and care. Problem of un-employment amongst young makes them unable to help financially.	No problem because of high rates of unem-ployment. But low wages and migration to other EU coun-tries may have knock on ef-fects. Plus fi-nancial prob-lems mean less people hired than needed.	Ditto – all levels can be em-ployed	Yes – Maltese Association helped start up a no of NGOs. Used in hos-pices	Very few for bet-ter off from Bye-lorussia.	1. no- very rare-Alzheimer groups 2. Yes for state instits. – not always in prac-tice, Not in pri-vate homes. 3. Yes -some
Portugal	Est. 2.3% of pop. cares for OP mainly women - 25% of FCs are male. Even when housekeeper employed, FC pays. supervi-sion, management, emo-tional support, transport and financial management.	High rate of female employ-ment – 61.2%	No problem. But problem of low earnings – limit choice available and the num-bers recruited	No – low earn-ings.	Few of the 50,000 work with OP – not attractive for volunteers. Informal sup-port from neighbours / friends. some local parish support thru' Catholic Church.	No official data. Influx from E.Europe, Ex Portuguese colo-nies cheaper and higher level of qualification esp. women as housekeepers. Medium and above income groups use housekeepers – mainly less inti-mate care of OP.	1. No 2. Heads of insti-tutions and services are qualified, not others. E.Europeans often more educated than locals of other migrants. 3. –

Country	Family carers	Trends in availability of FC / Combining work and care	Public services, labour supply and trends	Private services	Volunteers	Migrant carers	Training 1. family carers 2. formal carers 3. volunteers
						Legalised as domestic employees.	
Slovenia	FCs caring for 30-40,000 (10% of OP) (excluding those in institutions) Daughters, who were most frequently in touch with their parents, belonged to the 33 to 55-year age group and sons mostly to the 40 to 49-year age group. It has also been revealed that sisters, female pensioners, are also an important part of the informal network of the elderly	High rates of female employment but in 90s many at 50+ offered early retirement on full pension – which is no longer possible and will increase strain on FCs who work. *Act Amending the Social Security Act* not yet implemented but adopted, allows for FCs to be registered as 'family assistants'.	social carers numbers dropping due to insufficient funds to enable additional recruitment.	Available	Yes- growth in organizations providing volunteer support e.g. Red Cross, Caritas.	Not applicable	1. some 2. some 3. some
Spain	12.4% households contain a FC for the elderly. i.e., almost 5% of people over 18 give informal help to an OP approximate total of	75% of OP have more than one child alive (av. No nearly 3). Almost 24%	No information	Few emerging private organized services. Contracting private care	Very small participation of volunteers or the church in caring for	Immigrants, mainly illegal, important-, outside help is sought for a few	1. Some 2. Yes- full certification 3. some e.g. for Alzheimer,

Country	Family carers	Trends in availability of FC / Combining work and care	Public services, labour supply and trends	Private services	Volunteers	Migrant carers	Training 1. family carers 2. formal carers 3. volunteers
	1,464,299 people, of which 83% are women mainly 45-64 of low level education and housewife. 22% employed (36% part time work 64% full time. 28% of the population identifies an elderly person in their family in need of care and special attention, and almost 21% classify themselves as carers to some extent. FCs- spouse 12.4%, daughter 26%, son 15%, sister 1.4%, brother 0.4%, granddaughter 8%, grandson 5.4%, daughter-in-law 5.6%, son-in-law 6% other relatives 14%, neighbours and / or caretakers 5.6%, friends 4%, household employees under 1%.	share a home with some child and 43.5% live in the same town, But generational and L.M. changes especially for women, there is a feeling of uncertainty among current carers. They perceive a lack of reciprocity with respect to the coming generations of carers, and uncertainty as regards the future of those receiving care. Esp. acute among the older carers and those that are more alone 12% of FCs stopped work to deal with caring- Women without		associated with living alone (4X < chances of contracting it; absence of children. OP with high income and education leads to higher use of private service	the elderly (0.1%),	hours, but with increasing dependency stays in the home of OP Remain in this work until their situation is legalised. Problems: excessive working days, domestic activities beyond caring for the person, low wages, illegal situation. Balance is generally positive for the families and for the immigrant carers. Both positively value the affective relationships they establish with the OP.	some Regions.

Country	Family carers	Trends in availability of FC / Combining work and care	Public services, labour supply and trends	Private services	Volunteers	Migrant carers	Training 1. family carers 2. formal carers 3. volunteers
		studies or with primary education have a greater propensity to give up paid work.					
Sweden	"Rediscovery" of FC e.g. CARER 300 project 1. Increasing% OP relying on FC+ / -services, and declining% relying on public services+ / -FC 2. > 80% female LF participation. (highest in EU)	The integration of carer support into the formal service care management system.	Care workers (at all levels including physicians) major problems in recruitment and retention, many untrained and leaving LM (early retirement and sick leave) A high service system focusing on home care rather than institutional.	2 / 3 OP live alone. Public / private mix but private is not out-of-pocket payments	Voluntary orgs. Don't provide hands on care, but much informal volunteer help to OP – 3 nat. carers Orgs with public funding	No data	1. Yes – from subsidized carers' groups 2. Yes – in service – only half of 180,000 workers are trained in lower levels. 3. Yes- sit in services
Switzerland	23.1% of population aged 15+ have been caring - without payment - for a person aged 65+ in the year prior to survey = 1.36 mill persons. Pre-retired active pop. 50-59 years (36.9%) and young retirees 60-69 years (35.1%) provide more care than other age groups. more than 1 out	Few measures yet in place to support working FCs. Urban / rural and canton differences. Men aged 50-59 and 60-69 years old in equal proportions as FCs	Shortages of workers and migrants recruited to work in geriatric institutions and services.			Yes, especially women for domestic work. No data, currently being studied. Mainly from S. Europe and Latin America.	–

Country	Family carers	Trends in availability of FC Combining work and care	Public services, labour supply and trends	Private services	Volunteers	Migrant carers	Training 1. family carers 2. formal carers 3. volunteers
	of 4 older retirees aged 70-79 years old (26.3%) and of 40-49 years old (25.9%) provide care to another retiree.	F / T paid workers, students and disabled retirees report giving less care (still 11.9- 19.4% of FCs). 33% of retired, part time workers, working in the family company or at home report caring for an OP. 21.8% unemployed report providing care.					
UK	16% over the age of 16 are currently carers; 1 in 5 households contain a carer.= 6.8 million people in 5 million households Regional variations e.g. North East (20%) lowest in London (11%), 18-19% in N.W., S.W. and Wales. Peak of 24% at age 45-64, decreases to 16% aged 65+. FC women 18% V 14% men, no gender variations in the proportions of men and women who are co-resident carers. Women	None identified	Recruitment and retention a major issue with respect to both qualified and unqualified staff. In the former casework with older people is not accorded the value and status of acute care. With respect to unqualified staff, turnover is high	See public sector- same.	Large voluntary sector – many self help FC groups	No data on illegal migration. Migrants recruited and disproportionately employed in health and social services.	1. Yes- St. John's Ambulance- provide certification 2. NVQ qualifications for formal but not qualified professional carers. Formal professional carers are fully qualified and registered.

Country	Family carers	Trends in availability of FC / Combining work and care	Public services, labour supply and trends	Private services	Volunteers	Migrant carers	Training 1. family carers 2. formal carers 3. volunteers
	more likely to care for someone in another household (12% / 9%); to be the main supporter whether in the same (35% / 30%) or another household (25% / 19%); and to provide 20 hours or more care per week (29% / 26%). 52% are looking after a parent or parent-on-law, 16% are caring for a spouse, and 8% for a child One third of carers co-reside with the person they are caring for, while two thirds live in another household. Co-resident carers are more likely to be spending 20 hours a week or longer providing care (63% / 11%). Spouses are majority of co-resident FCs especially 75+.		and wages low, further exacerbating an already difficult situation				3. Yes

5.10 Annex 10 – Matrix: Other Issues

Countries	Health and Well-being of FC	Abuse in FC situations	Carers groups	Hours of care, Responsibility for FC	New technologies	Property and inheritance & reciprocity
Austria	69% FC said physical burdens; 79% psychological burdens; social isolation severe problem	–	Pensioners' organizations affiliated to political parties. Umbrella organization	-	Low IT usage by OP. Medical alert or alarm systems as a personal emergency response system but few covered - 0.2% of all people aged 65 years or over.	72% of FC felt transfers were important. And only 28% felt that inheritance plays "a negligible role" in intergenerational relations.
Belgium		1998 setting up of Central Report Point for Elderly Abuse and Centre for help for mistreated elderly people)	Yes, important.		2002-3 20% men, 9% women 65-74 used IT (9% M, 2% W Internet) www.seniorweb.be provides information, organizes computer courses for elderly people and internet panel discussions on topics that concern OP and FCs.	No role
Bulgaria	No data	-		-	-	Yes play a part. State intervenes if family take property of Op and then do not provide care.
Czech Republic			Only a few, but several strong NGOs of	-	Some home alarm systems operated	Not legally

Countries	Health and Well-being of FC	Abuse in FC situations	Carers groups	Hours of care, Responsibility for FC	New technologies	Property and inheritance & reciprocity
			OP who provide some services that also help FCs. Alzheimer Association an exception		by Zivot 90 and the Centre of Gerontology. Czech Alzheimer Society has database of services see www.gerontologie.cz	
Denmark	1 small study showed FCs esp. ageing spouses providing care and support are concerned about their own health and well-being and worry about what would happen if they could no longer care for the spouse.	No data -	Yes one to support cooperation between FCs and professionals. www.pgruppen.dk - Relatives of Frail Older People but other NGOs (2) also support OP and FCs	less than 1% in 1 study got help from family members or other members of social networks with personal care that less than 5% aged 60-75 years live with children. LA obliged to provide respite help to spouses, parents or other close relatives caring for a physically or mentally disabled person.		Unlikely
Finland	-	Absence of data	3 main groups – largest national wide, bi-lingual. Funded by slot machines Association. 1 focuses on caregivers	1 / 3 60+ get some help	Yes gerotechnology e.g. locomotion devices in / out of house, eating, sleeping, security e.g. timers for lights, locomotion recognition, security telephone, doorbell	No. Increase in OP living alone. 60% of 75+ live in 1 person households.

Countries	Health and Well-being of FC	Abuse in FC situations	Carers groups	Hours of care, Responsibility for FC	New technologies	Property and inheritance & reciprocity
					alarm. For FC nigh alarm- wakes FC up if OP moves from bed in night,	
France	Risks of depression is twice higher Amongst FCs than in the general population.	Debate on maltreatment and abuse of OP in institutions and at home by informal and professional carers	2- but not very strong in terms of impact.	No data. Old parents - 50% have 1 child nearby (less 1 km.), and 90% a child living < 50 km; 31% are living in the same village or town and 67% in the same Depart.	Yes, but no data e.g. use > mobile phones and Internet by 50+. Websites on socio-gerontology with info and advice for FCs. New technologies have an indirect impact on FCs- thru alarms	Probably but no data / research
Germany	Study of 1911 FCs- those who spend large amounts of time reported physical complaints such as exhaustion, pain in arms and legs, heart trouble and severe stomach pain more than for general population. symptoms more pronounced in FCs of cognitively impaired persons	10,8% (n=46) reported violence, whereas psychological maltreatment and financial damage were reported more frequently. - related to > need for support and care + a decline of physical strength. Domestic violence hidden. OW more often the victims of domestic abuse But FCs acting violently towards their OP only 22%	2 major Foundations and many NGOs, pressure groups and FC groups but 6% regularly visit coffee-groups for FCs or counselling hours. 2% meet in private self-help groups and 3% regularly meet in groups for family carers with professional counselling. Only about 16% of all FCs regularly and 37% occasion-	62% of OP live in the same household with FC, 8% FCs live in the same house or very nearby, about 14% live less than 10 minutes away, about 8% live more than 10 minutes away, remaining 8% of OP in need of regular family care-giving or support. Amongst terminally	Yes gerotechnology promoted in LA centers or charitable organisations and the gerotechnological industry pro-vides the exhibits mostly for free because there is a great interest in selling new technologies e.g. "Skala-mobiles", complete barrier-free furnishing, emergency-calls, adapting sanitary	Yes important- study showed that 42% people believed social-normative obligations for FC-giving is purely altruistic. Moral obligations and financial considerations are not mutually exclusive.

Countries	Health and Well-being of FC	Abuse in FC situations	Carers groups	Hours of care, Responsibility for FC	New technologies	Property and inheritance & reciprocity
		of all reported cases of abuse against OP. Also unknown no. of cases of abuse of OP against FCs.	ally take up counselling and advice.	ill > 81% FCs were female: wives, daughters or daughters in law. 32% of these FCs were also in paid employment and for daughters proportion was 61%!; 87% of them additionally were responsible for their own household	environment or several appliances in order to balance functional handicaps or impairments.	
Greece	No data. Small old qualitative study of 24 FCs, 8 had bad health, 11 deteriorating health. 7 clinical depression. Only 3 no psychological problems. 50% mentioned positive aspects of care.	data from 1989 – known financial and emotional abuse in some cases	Virtually no general carers' groups and no representation at national level. Existing ones are for carers of those with Alzheimer- over 20 of these.	No data. 42% of all FCs assess to be rather heavy and 41% of FCs extremely physically and mentally burdened and only 7% assessed no to be burdened	mobile telephone has helped communications between FC and OP. Low rates of Internet connection amongst OP.	Yes- reciprocity important. Property often transferred at marriage of children, with parents having usage.
Hungary	30-50% of people in the 70-79 years age group, and maj of OP > 80 years need help in day-to-day activities	No data. Pre 1990 the practice of contracts for support gave opportunities for abuse against the elderly. Today one of the greatest problems is robbery of the elderly.	The large NGOs work to support and train FCs.	80% of OP counted on FC in official affairs, household tasks and nursing. Fewer can count on financial help	Alarm bell systems – low tech but affordable and linked OP to families and neighbours throughout country. social and family connections of the elderly	Yes – private ownership as a resource for OP that they can pass on to children. Reciprocity and gifts from parent to child throughout life.
Ireland	Overload has nega-		Yes 4.	½ in separate	70 community	Reciprocity a de-

Countries	Health and Well-being of FC	Abuse in FC situations	Carers groups	Hours of care, Responsibility for FC	New technologies	Property and inheritance & reciprocity
	tive effect on physical & mental well being – at risk groups for own health. 24% FC in poor health, 30% thought health has suffered, 25% injured.		Caring for Carers- 69 groups, Carers Assoc- 16 groups, + 2 others.	households. Hours increase with dependency. 76.8% care for 1 person, 19.8% for 2. 3,4% for 3+ 1-19 hrs- 60.3% FC 13.4% - 30-49 hrs. 26.7% - 50 hrs +.	based projects supported Community Application of IT – Caring for Carers initiated IT project with Mid Western Health Board, CICentre Ennis and Ennis I Age Town. Target group 1500 not yet mainstreamed. Poorly developed and poor legislation. Internet for shopping.	bate – increasing role of grandparents. in child care Only anecdotally. Inheritance of home – Issue whether family home + other assets should be taken into consideration for funding LTC.
Italy	-	Elder abuse discussed with ref to residential homes but less so about FC. Results on FCs feeling tyrannised by OP also apparent (spouses and daughters especially mention this).	2 major Alzheimer groups working nationally. A.U.S.E.R. (NGO for elderly care) recently published a "manifesto of carers' rights" and a national conference on "Supporting carers for the rights of the persons cared for"		High cost, mainly privately paid - Security alarm systems, video-telephones, mechanized shutter lock, tele-medicine devices, transponder or mechanised door (or window) opener, data network (for rapid shared access to Internet), bedroom intercom, visual and auditory signals, remote control apparatus of	Problems of guardianship of OP property if they are not able to look after themselves.

Countries	Health and Well-being of FC	Abuse in FC situations	Carers groups	Hours of care, Responsibility for FC	New technologies	Property and inheritance & reciprocity
					certain functions via phone, SMS or Internet, Internet websites for FCs mainly dedicated to families of Alzheimer's and psychiatric patients.	
Luxembourg	No data.	No data	No – Alzheimer Society of LU partly and many organizations including NGOs for them but not of them. But there are 3 organizations of senior citizens.	35% of dependent people needed in excess of 24 hours per week. Mean time was 21.2 hours. – this has increased. 3.5hrs-13.99-38.5% 14-23.99 – 26.5 24-33.99 – 20.8 34-43.99 – 7.4 44-63.99 – 4.6 64-83.5 – 2.1 But this coves younger people – and more time needed by younger (19-40) since handicapped. But next group are those aged 90+, then 80-89, 70-79.	Tele Alarm, Senior hot lines provide information Luxembourg programmes and web site www.luxsenior.lu	?
Malta	No studies- 1 done	-	No carers groups,	-	Telecare	The majority of

Countries	Health and Well-being of FC	Abuse in FC situations	Carers groups	Hours of care, Responsibility for FC	New technologies	Property and inheritance & reciprocity
	with 100 FCs for this report. 65.6 per cent of the interviewed family carers replied that they spend whole day in the care of their OP,		there are pensioners organizations		Service links OP with FCs.	Malta's elderly persons bequeath their property to the child who takes care of them when they become dependent. Deep embedment in family support networks of interdependence, of giving and receiving. OP are a boon to their working children e.g. financial assistance, baby sitting, etc, conflict resolution.
Netherlands	150-200,000 FCs over / burdened if partner or spouse because care involves care for 24 / 7 / 12, more often deprived of income, use less services for FCs. FCs under 65 have more trouble combining work and care when providing personal care and / or psychosocial or emotional support.	11% of FCs of OP with dementia had engaged in physical aggression. 30% of FCs reported chronic verbal aggression	Many such groups including support centers for informal carers (and the national organization for these support centers Xzorg), voluntary (terminal) home care organizations, organization for informal caregivers (LOT), and the Expertise center for Informal Care (EIZ).	2,4 million people 19% of the Dutch population over 18 years provide FC at least 3 months + or 8+ hrs per week. 400,000 (18.8% of all FC) intense care for 65+, 830,000 long term less intense. Av. FC help for 17.9 hours per week FC give domestic help (75%) psychosocial sup-	Houses are created in which people can live throughout their whole lifespan with alarm systems, ICT-technology etc. Some professional home care organisations are offering computer technologies for older people and their caregivers to ask nurses by the use of webcams and internet ques-	No data

Countries	Health and Well-being of FC	Abuse in FC situations	Carers groups	Hours of care, Responsibility for FC	New technologies	Property and inheritance & reciprocity
	.			port (81%), personal care (34%), though for terminally ill FCs provide much personal assistance (66%). 67% of FCs give multiple forms of care. 40% FCs without assistance 60% get help from secondary informal caregivers.	tions about care	
Norway	FC spouses of OP with dementia found that the majority report negative effects of caregiving on their own health	Estimated as between 3% and 6% - studies in the Nordic countries abuse of elderly varies from 1% to 8%. More frequent experiences of violence by middle and OW in cities. (5%) than country.	Voluntary organisations for elderly and for FCs to give information and support as well as being watch dogs and co-operating agents in relation to the formal service system. 13% (but rising nos of) LAs had established support groups for caregivers; fewer had special courses, training or consultation services for caregivers.	Study of complete cohort from age 80 to the death of each cohort member showed total no. of years of FC received by women was on average 8.8 years and for men 5.3 years (i.e. after the care receiver reached the age of 80). Hrs of informal care to older (and disabled) people increase with age of caregiver, with a peak for middle aged women (aged 45-66 years) Women give 2.5	There are Offices for Assistive Aids in every County. Safety alarms and other equipment are widely used by elderly and their carers.	Yes- considerable transfers from OP as inheritance, pre-inheritance and gifts though this is shown not to influence the amount of care given to older parents by children - generally. If parents are in need of nursing, previous help from parents to children result in more nursing by children, and most so for fathers Elderly in general give more help and economic support to the younger genera-

Countries	Health and Well-being of FC	Abuse in FC situations	Carers groups	Hours of care, Responsibility for FC	New technologies	Property and inheritance & reciprocity
				times as much f. c. as men. women give more help than men do to other households – no differences within same household.		tions, compared to the help they receive. For mothers amount of help received also depends on whether she had helped her children
Poland	No data	No data. Extreme cases in some private homes.	Not FCs. Pensioners' organizations affiliated to political parties.	No national data. Where co resident difficult to measure – some studies have suggested 100 hours a week,	No data	Yes- legally controlled. Importance of reciprocity – esp. since so many are co-resident, and support of Op pension for unemployed.
Portugal	56.1% depression (26.5% severe, moderate) Needs and problems vary by income levels – leisure an issue for the better off, financial help for the worse off.	No accurate data. Research reveals very little – mainly emotional or psychological abuse. (affective blackmail by both parties)	No rep. groups of FCs. Some Alzheimer, Parkinson groups. Where they exist NGOs are effective in improving local initiatives and provisions. (e.g. training, support in kind, self help)	39% care alone, 61% have support from social agencies, relatives or housekeeper. 68.3% care for more than 4 hours p.d.. 56.6% care every day, 6.9% occasionally, 17.2% FC relies on formal support, 6.9% have rotational care.	Green Paper 1997 to favour disadvantaged in Inf. Soc. Network of disabled and elderly, Min. of science and Technology offers free Internet. Portugal Telecom (text, text phone, Grid. emergency terminal with free hand phone.. Alarm Service., portable amplifier, luminous call sign, discounts,	Not property, but exchange of goods and services and reciprocity

Countries	Health and Well-being of FC	Abuse in FC situations	Carers groups	Hours of care, Responsibility for FC	New technologies	Property and inheritance & reciprocity
					financial facilities in gaining access to equipment.	
Slovenia	FCs very isolated and high bodily and physical strains (27.3%). No spare *time* (15%) and less *time for their family* (10%). FCs most miss financial help and home help; the third place occupied by help in accommodation of OP in OP home 45.8% carers did not know who to turn to for help.	½ OP abused by their children. Family members or relatives were responsible for three quarters of incidences of abuse. FCs commit abuse because they are so worn out. 10,9% from institution where they lived.	Not per se but strong NGOs – esp. Pensioners Associations	> 2 / 3 OP received help from close relatives several times a week and a50% every day. Some FCs caring for 2 persons. FC. 52.5% caring for their parents for over 6 years and 1 / 3 for > 10 years. < 1 / 3 for up to one year. Type of help by FCs- handling finance (80% rs), household tasks (75%), accompanying (70%), help with nutrition (62.5%) nursing and personal hygiene (55%). latter provided by different persons – children (53.6%), other close relatives (39.3%) and home nurses (28.6%)	'Red button', tele-alarm system of the Home help centre offering help to people in a health crisis and the lonely ones is not gaining users despite heavy investments into it.	Critical importance of reciprocity – esp. currently where high unemployment rates and families get support from OP. Can be misused where FC is not a relative... However OP unwilling to see large apartments since they wish to leave property to their children- so won't pay for care.
Spain	Combining FC and working out of home negative health effects.- increase in	Only academic debate – no resonance,	Yes. Especially Alzheimer' groups – subsidized by govt.	56% of FCs provide daily care; 22% every week, 14% occasional. Mostly	Tele-assistance was given to less than 1% of the elder	63% of FCs indicate that OP do not given them an economic reward, 23%

Countries	Health and Well-being of FC	Abuse in FC situations	Carers groups	Hours of care, Responsibility for FC	New technologies	Property and inheritance & reciprocity
	morbidity, worsens perception of health status, and increases use of HSs. 64% FCs less leisure, 51% tired, 48% no holiday, 39% no visit to friends, 32% depressed, 29% health deteriorated, 27% can't work, 26% No time to look after other people, 23% no time for themselves, 21% financial problems, 12% reduced their working day, 12% gave up work, 9% conflicts with partner. 71,4% of main carers psychologically not well		OP in associations of pensioners or widows also subsidised publicly or by non profit-making entities, intended to encourage the elderly to lead an active life and to offer them a medium for socialising.	all day or two hours a day FC spends av. 7 hrs a day caring, and may receive help one hour a day. From rest of network High% of OP in Spain report fair to bad health 59% live together permanently, 16% live together temporarily, 26% live in separate dwellings or in other forms – large urban / rural variations in living alone for OP.	Internet growing- for FCs "The Experts Centre" experiment to resolve problems in caring for the elderly, sponsored by the Red Cross and the Obra Social de Caja Madrid. A website offering a consulting service Users are able to find free professional advice on e.g. health, meals, advice on legal and business matters, volunteer force, addiction etc.	regularly receive compensation and 13% do from time to time. Negative perception of the impact of caring on the family economy but an expense especially in families with a medium-low economic status, since pensions are low and does not cover the costs they cause
Sweden	No data	No data though recognized as a problem especially where caring forced on FC -	Yes - 3 main groups growing in importance - Dementia Association (1984) has about 12 000 members and 110 local organisations in most areas; The Alzheimer Associa-	No data	3 Yr action plan (1999-2001) stimulating LAs to develop an infrastructure of services targeting family caregivers. The plan funded LAs to expand services for	No data though assets of different kinds play a role in the negotiation of family obligation

Countries	Health and Well-being of FC	Abuse in FC situations	Carers groups	Hours of care, Responsibility for FC	New technologies	Property and inheritance & reciprocity
			tion Sweden, (1987. the Carers Sweden, 1996 - national umbrella organisation, and to promote carers' interest on a broad scale, through advocacy-, information- and awareness raising activities.		carers e.g. by setting up caregiver resource centres that offer training, counselling, support groups, respite care, information and resources for family caregivers, including day programs for their disabled family members. The experiences and outcome of the Carer-300 project has been systematically followed and evaluated the recent years. ACTION telematics intervention programme used with 40 families is successful.	
Switzerland	Study comparing N and S cantons showed differences 40% reported depression, 26% of Basel FCs & 18% of FCs in Ticino showed depressive symptoms. In Basel,	Under examined but n NGO exists to deal with abuse.	Yes- for Alzheimer and other /	Majority FCs provide 3 - 20 hrs p.m., the peak duration being 6-10 hrs care p.m. Women spend only a very slight amount of time more than men p.w. 16.4% of men and		

Countries	Health and Well-being of FC	Abuse in FC situations	Carers groups	Hours of care, Responsibility for FC	New technologies	Property and inheritance & reciprocity
	up to 70% of FCs indicated health-related problems.			18.9% of women give 21 hours + for FC p.m. Members of the family provide an average of 17.9 hours of care per week over a mean duration of 6.5 years		
UK	Differences in labour market incomes after episodes of care 2 / 3 or 4 years not different from those not involved in care over these intervals, but longer episodes related to larger gaps in incomes between carers and non-carers. with six or	2,400 complaints made to Action on Elder Abuse 50% approx by relatives, 28% by a paid worker, 11% by a friend of the victim, most cases taking place in the victim's own home. According to the survey, one in three old one in five is physically abused and the same number have their savings inappropriately used; more than 10% are neglected and 2.4% sexually abused	Carers UK led by carers with National and regional offices 114. Income from public grants (36%) 19% donations from trusts and public bodies, 15% from legacies, 6% from corporate donations and sponsorship, and 4% from membership subscriptions. Princess Royal Trust for Carers – 113 networks. Offer grants and training. Crossroads Caring for Carers – 202 centres – for breaks to 39,000 carers	4 million carers work and care (1 / 9 women and 1 / 10 men combining work with the support of a frail older person	Social Services may provide text phones, flashing or vibrating alarm clocks or door bells and loop systems for listening to the television. Disabled living centres provide advice and access to mod. Support technologies in UK e.g. Environmental control systems,, PCs, CD-Roms and ISDN lines provide OP and FCs with access to information.	When someone goes into a residential home they may be required to sell their home, so individuals who are likely to benefit from the inheritance of property may be influenced in their decision to care for their elderly relative.

Countries	Health and Well-being of FC	Abuse in FC situations	Carers groups	Hours of care, Responsibility for FC	New technologies	Property and inheritance & reciprocity
			with paid, trained care staff.			

155

Gerontologie

hrsg. von Hanneli Döhner
(Universität Hamburg)

Christopher Kofahl; Katharina Dahl;
Hanneli Döhner
**Vernetzte Versorgung für ältere
Menschen in Deutschland**
Schon seit vielen Jahren bestehen bundesweit Initiativen und Projekte, die sich einer koordinierten gesundheitlichen und sozialen Versorgung älterer Patienten widmen. In dem Buch sind viele gute Ansätze zusammengetragen und systematisierend dargestellt worden. Es bietet einen Fundus an Anregungen, mit welchen Mitteln eine besser koordinierte Versorgung bei älteren Menschen erreicht werden könnte. Schließlich wird deutlich gemacht, dass die wissenschaftliche Nachweislage bezüglich Wirksamkeit und Nutzen der oft aufwändigen Interventionen wie z.B. beim Case-Management noch unbefriedigend ist
Bd. 8, 2004, 120 S., 12,90 €, br.,
ISBN 3-8258-8195-4

Hanneli Döhner; Thomas Stamm
(Hg.)
**Geriatrische Qualifizierung für
Hausärzte**
Entwicklung, Erprobung und Evaluation eines interdisziplinären Fortbildungskonzeptes
Der Hausarzt sichert die ärztliche Versorgung älterer und hilfsbedürftiger Menschen zuhause, in ihrem gewohnten sozialen Umfeld und in Einrichtungen der teil- und vollstationären Pflege. Er ist der wesentliche ambulante Ansprechpartner für ältere Menschen und der wichtigste ärztliche Kooperationspartner der ambulanten Pflegedienste. Trotz dieser Schlüsselrolle des Hausarztes in der Begleitung und Behandlung ist die hausärztliche Fortbildung in den zentralen Themen der Geriatrie bisher unzureichend.
Bd. 9, 2005, 120 S., 7,90 €, br.,
ISBN 3-8258-8534-8

Erlanger Beiträge zur Gerontologie

hrsg. von Prof. Dr. Wolf D. Oswald
und Prof. Dr. Heinz J. Kaiser

Heinz Jürgen Kaiser (Hg.)
Autonomie und Kompetenz
Aspekte einer gerontologischen Herausforderung
Die Autonomie und Kompetenz der Menschen bis ins hohe Alter hinein zu bewahren, das ist eine der großen gesellschaftlichen Herausforderungen in den Industriestaaten des 21. Jahrhunderts. Zugleich umreißt dieses Ziel die entscheidende Aufgabe der anwendungsorientierten gerontologischen Forschung unserer Zeit. Große Fortschritte wurden bereits mit dem Erlanger Forschungsprojekt SIMA („Selbstständigkeit im Alter") gemacht. 20 renommierte Vertreter der deutschen Gerontologie behandeln aus der Position unterschiedlicher gerontologischer Disziplinen Aspekte der von SIMA behandelten Thematik und sind gleichsam als Kommentare zu Fragestellungen und Ergebnissen des Projekts zu lesen.
Bd. 1, 2003, 296 S., 30,90 €, br.,
ISBN 3-8258-6150-3

Christine M. Augst
Selbstreflexionen im höheren Lebensalter
Inhalte und Strukturen von Lebensbetrachtungen
Im höheren Lebensalter werden Selbstreflexionen insbesondere durch die hier

LIT Verlag Münster – Berlin – Hamburg – London – Wien
Grevener Str./Fresnostr. 2 48159 Münster
Tel.: 0251 – 62 032 22 – Fax: 0251 – 23 19 72
e-Mail: vertrieb@lit-verlag.de – http://www.lit-verlag.de

charakteristischen physischen, psychischen und sozialen Veränderungen angestoßen. Es werden Inhalte und Funktionen von Vergangenheits-, Gegenwarts- und Zukunftsbetrachtungen dargestellt und im Zusammenhang mit Sinnerleben, Identitätsstabilisierung sowie Bewältigung kritischer Lebensereignisse besprochen. Die Bedeutung, die biographische Ereignisse, aktuelle Lebensbedingungen und individuelle Interpretationsstile für die Lebensbetrachtungen alter Menschen haben, wird durch eine empirische Analyse untermauert.

Bd. 2, 2003, 200 S., 19,90 €, br.,
ISBN 3-8258-6771-4

Stefan Blüher
Integration und Solidarität
Pflege im Alter – theoretische Überlegungen, empirische Befunde und praktische Konsequenzen
Der fortschreitende demographische Wandel und veränderte Formen privaten Zusammenlebens sind Entwicklungen, die Fragen von sozialer Integration und Solidarität unmittelbar berühren. Angesichts dieser Wandlungsprozesse treten neue Integrationserfordernisse auf, die mit den etablierten Formen kollektiver Sicherung nicht mehr angemessen beantwortet werden können. Ein Beispiel für Integration und Solidarität unter dergestalt veränderten Rahmenbedingungen ist die soziale Teilabsicherung im Rahmen der Pflegeversicherung, die in ihren mikro- und makrosozialen Auswirkungen empirisch beleuchtet wird.

Bd. 3, 2005, 272 S., 18,90 €, br.,
ISBN 3-8258-8421-x

Andreas Ackermann
Empirische Untersuchungen in der stationären Altenhilfe
Relevanz und methodische Besonderheiten der gerontologischen Interventionsforschung mit Pflegeheimbewohnern
Qualitätssicherung und Evidenzbasierung sind Begriffe, die auch im Bereich der stationären Altenhilfe immer stärker an Bedeutung gewinnen. Personelle und finanzielle Ressourcen sind zu knapp bemessen, als dass man auf die Überprüfung der Wirksamkeit von sinnvollen und dringend notwendigen Maßnahmen für Pflegeheimbewohner wie z.B. der Prävention und Rehabilitation verzichten könnte. Dieses Buch zeigt Möglichkeiten und Grenzen der empirischen Arbeit mit Pflegeheimbewohnern und ist somit an Praktiker, Wissenschaftler und vor allem auch die Empfänger von Ergebnissen derartiger Untersuchungen gerichtet.

Bd. 4, 2005, 248 S., 22,90 €, br.,
ISBN 3-8258-8579-8

Medizin und Gesellschaft

Klaus Sames; Sebastian Sethe; Alexandra Stolzing (Eds.)
Extending the Lifespan
Biotechnical, Gerontological, and Social Problems. Collected transcripts of the international conference on "Experimental gerontology", conducted by the German Society of Gerontology and Geriatrics (DGGG e. V. Sektion I), 24–26th September 2003, Hamburg, Germany
This book collects the essays and presentations that were the product of a highly successful international meeting on experimental gerontology, conducted by

LIT Verlag Münster – Berlin – Hamburg – London – Wien
Grevener Str./Fresnostr. 2 48159 Münster
Tel.: 0251 – 62 032 22 – Fax: 0251 – 23 19 72
e-Mail: vertrieb@lit-verlag.de – http://www.lit-verlag.de

the German Society for Gerontology and Gerontology in September 2003. In this volume, specialists from a variety of backgrounds address a multitude of issues including: *Theories of Aging – Analytical Gerontology – Nutrition and Lifespan – Antioxidants – Genetic Repair – Life Extension Mathematics – Tissue Engineering – Transplantation – Stem Cells – Cryopreservation – Nanotechnology – Criminology – Ethics in Research and Care*

Bd. 12, 2005, 264 S., 39,90 €, gb.,
ISBN 3-8258-8563-1

Dortmunder Beiträge zur Sozial- und Gesellschaftspolitik

hrsg. von Prof. Dr. Gerhard Naegele (Universität Dortmund) und Dr. Gerd Peter (Landesinstitut Sozialforschungsstelle Dortmund)

Gerhard Bäcker; Rolf G. Heinze; Gerhard Naegele
Die Sozialen Dienste vor neuen Herausforderungen
Bd. 1, 1995, 240 S., 20,90 €, br.,
ISBN 3-8258-2579-5

Bernhard Rosendahl
Bericht zur sozialen Lage älterer Menschen in Dortmund
im Auftrag des Landesinstituts Sozialforschungsstelle Dortmund
Bd. 2, 1995, 296 S., 20,90 €, br.,
ISBN 3-8258-2550-7

Frerich Frerichs (Hg.)
Älterer Arbeitnehmer im Demographischen Wandel – Qualifizierungsmodelle und Eingliederungsstrategien
Bd. 7, 1996, 200 S., 19,90 €, br.,
ISBN 3-8258-2725-9

Monika Reichert;
Gerhard Naegele (Hrsg.)
Alterssicherung in Nordrhein-Westfalen: Daten und Fakten
Bd. 11, 1997, 312 S., 25,90 €, br.,
ISBN 3-8258-3186-8

Thomas Kauss, Sabine Kühnert, Gerhard Naegele, Waldemar Schmidt, Eckart Schnabel
Vernetzung in der ambulanten geriatrischen Versorgung – die Schlüsselstellung des Hausarztes
Bd. 16, 1998, 304 S., 25,90 €, br.,
ISBN 3-8258-3648-7

Monika Reichert (Hg.)
Häusliche Pflege in Nordrhein-Westfalen
Bd. 17, 1998, 296 S., 25,90 €, br.,
ISBN 3-8258-3675-4

Dietmar Köster
Strukturwandel und Weiterbildung älterer Menschen
Eine Studie des neuen alters im Auftrag der Hans-Böckler-Stiftung und des Ministeriums für Arbeit, Gesundheit und Soziales NRW
Bd. 18, 1998, 216 S., 17,90 €, br.,
ISBN 3-8258-3881-1

Katrin Krämer
Betriebliche Gesundheitsförderung
Konzeption. Wirkungen. Evaluation
Bd. 19, 1998, 152 S., 17,90 €, br.,
ISBN 3-8258-3963-x

LIT Verlag Münster – Berlin – Hamburg – London – Wien
Grevener Str./Fresnostr. 2 48159 Münster
Tel.: 0251 – 62 032 22 – Fax: 0251 – 23 19 72
e-Mail: vertrieb@lit-verlag.de – http://www.lit-verlag.de

Christine Fromm
Betrieblicher Gesundheitsschutz und soziale Selbstverwaltung
Gestaltungsaufgaben und Handlungsmöglichkeiten der Sozialen Selbstverwaltung im Zusammenhang mit der aktuellen Strukturreform des betrieblichen Gesundheitsschutzes
Bd. 21, 1999, 184 S., 17,90 €, br.,
ISBN 3-8258-4146-4

Bernhard Rosendahl
Kommunalisierung und korporative Vernetzung in der Implementation der Pflegeversicherung
Wirkungsanalyse regionaler Pflegekonferenzen in Nordrhein-Westfalen
Bd. 22, 1999, 320 S., 25,90 €, br.,
ISBN 3-8258-4195-2

Arno Georg; Frerich Frerichs
Ältere Arbeitnehmer in NRW
Betriebliche Problemfelder und Handlungsansätze
Bd. 24, 1999, 216 S., 20,90 €, br.,
ISBN 3-8258-4399-8

Gerhard Naegele; Gerd Peter (Hg.)
Arbeit – Alter – Region
Zur Debatte um die Zukunft der Arbeit, um die demographische Entwicklung und die Chancen regionalpolitischer Gestaltung. Beiträge aus FfG und sfs
Bd. 25, 2000, 304 S., 20,90 €, br.,
ISBN 3-8258-4247-9

Petra Bröscher
Gewalt – Erfahrungen im Leben alternder Frauen
Bd. 26, 1999, 160 S., 15,90 €, br.,
ISBN 3-8258-4354-8

Marion Vortmann
Freiwilliges Engagement älterer Menschen als Instrument der gesellschaftlichen Partizipation
Handlungsbedarf und Förderstrategien
Bd. 33, 2001, 164 S., 17,90 €, br.,
ISBN 3-8258-5406-x

Nicole Maly
Töchter, die ihre Mütter pflegen
Eine Analyse ihrer Lebenssituation
Bd. 34, 2001, 224 S., 20,90 €, br.,
ISBN 3-8258-5519-8

Gerhard Naegele; Monika Reichert; Nicole Maly
10 Jahre Gerontologische Forschung in Dortmund
Bilanz und Perspektiven
Bd. 35, 2001, 136 S., 15,90 €, br.,
ISBN 3-8258-5541-4

Wolf Klehm (Hg.)
Das ZWAR-Konzept
Moderation, Animation und existentielle Begegnung in der Gruppenarbeit mit "Jungen Alten". Rekonstruktion und Reflexion auf der Grundlage ethnographischer Bildungsforschung
Bd. 36, 2002, 256 S., 20,90 €, br.,
ISBN 3-8258-5814-6

Eckart Schnabel; Frauke Schönberg (Hg.)
Qualitätsentwicklung in der Versorgung Pflegebedürftiger
Bilanz und Perspektiven
Bd. 41, 2003, 240 S., 17,90 €, br.,
ISBN 3-8258-6632-7

LIT Verlag Münster – Berlin – Hamburg – London – Wien
Grevener Str./Fresnostr. 2 48159 Münster
Tel.: 0251 – 62 032 22 – Fax: 0251 – 23 19 72
e-Mail: vertrieb@lit-verlag.de – http://www.lit-verlag.de

Monika Reichert;
Angela Carell; Maggie Pearson;
Andrew Nocon (Hg.)
Informelle außerfamiliäre Unterstützungsnetzwerke älterer Menschen mit Hilfe- und Pflegebedarf
Eine deutsch-britische Vergleichsstudie
Bd. 45, 2003, 136 S., 14,90 €, br.,
ISBN 3-8258-7028-6

Frerich Frerichs; Kai Leichsenring;
Gerhard Naegele; Monika Reichert;
Michael Stadler-Vida
Qualität Sozialer Dienste in Deutschland und Österreich
Bd. 49, 2003, 264 S., 19,90 €, br.,
ISBN 3-8258-7191-6

Andrea Kuhlmann
Case Management für demenzkranke Menschen
Eine Betrachtung der gegenwärtigen praktischen Umsetzung
Die Realisierung einer umfassenden ambulanten Versorgung ist – insbesondere für demenziell erkrankte Menschen, die überwiegend zu Hause durch Angehörige gepflegt werden – in einem Versorgungssystem, das durch Unübersichtlichkeit und fehlende Vernetzung gekennzeichnet ist, oftmals erschwert. Angesichts dessen wird seit ca. zehn Jahren der Einsatz von Case Management in der Altenhilfe favorisiert. Inwiefern Case Management zu einer bedarfsgerechten Versorgung demenzkranker Menschen beitragen kann und welche Bedeutung Case Management gegenwärtig im Rahmen des Modellprojektes „Persönliches Pflegebudget" zukommt, wird im vorliegenden Band diskutiert.
Bd. 54, 2005, 216 S., 20,90 €, br.,
ISBN 3-8258-8482-1

Frank Bauer; Hermann Groß;
Georg Sieglen; Michael Schwarz
Betriebszeit- und Arbeitszeitmanagement
Ergebnisse einer repräsentativen Betriebsbefragung in Europa
In diesem Buch wird eine Analyse des Betriebszeit- und Arbeitszeitmanagements in sechs europäischen Ländern (Großbritannien, Deutschland, Frankreich, die Niederlande, Portugal und Spanien) vorgestellt. Zusätzlich wurde Nordrhein-Westfalen in diese Analyse einbezogen. Diese Analyse basiert auf einer repräsentativen Betriebsbefragung, die in allen Untersuchungsländern mit einem einheitlichen Fragebogen und einheitlichen Verfahren der Messung und Berechnung der Daten durchgeführt wurde, um den strengen Kriterien der internationalen Vergleichbarkeit Rechnung zu tragen. Dieses Projekt („EUCOWE") wurde von der Europäischen Kommission im Kontext des 5. Forschungsrahmenprogramms finanziell gefördert.
Bd. 55, Herbst 2005, ca. 184 S., ca. 19,90 €, br.,
ISBN 3-8258-8941-6

LIT Verlag Münster – Berlin – Hamburg – London – Wien
Grevener Str./Fresnostr. 2 48159 Münster
Tel.: 0251 – 62 03 22 – Fax: 0251 – 23 19 72
e-Mail: vertrieb@lit-verlag.de – http://www.lit-verlag.de